Architecting Complex-Event Processing Solutions with TIBCO®

TIBCO® Press

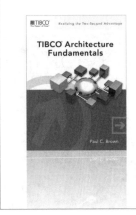

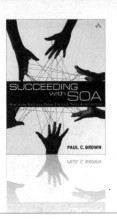

Addison-Wesley

Visit informit.com/tibcopress for a complete list of available publications.

TIBCO® Press provides books to help users of TIBCO technology design and build real-world solutions. The initial books – the architecture series – provide practical guidance for building solutions by combining components from TIBCO's diverse product suite. Each book in the architecture series covers an application area from three perspectives: a conceptual overview, a survey of applicable TIBCO products, and an exploration of common design challenges and TIBCO-specific design patterns for addressing them. The first book in the series, *TIBCO® Architecture Fundamentals*, addresses the basics of SOA and event-driven architectures. Each of the advanced books addresses a particular architecture style, including composite applications and services, complex event processing, business process management, and data-centric solutions.

The series emphasizes the unification of business process and system design in an approach known as *total architecture*. A technology-neutral description of this approach to distributed systems architecture is described in *Implementing SOA: Total Architecture in Practice*. Techniques for addressing the related organizational and management issues are described in *Succeeding with SOA: Realizing Business Value through Total Architecture*.

Make sure to connect with us!
informit.com/socialconnect

Addison
Wesley

informIT.com
THE TRUSTED TECHNOLOGY LEARNING SOURCE

Safari
Books Online

Architecting Complex-Event Processing Solutions with TIBCO®

Paul C. Brown

∧⩔Addison-Wesley

Upper Saddle River, NJ • Boston • Indianapolis • San Francisco
New York • Toronto • Montreal • London • Munich • Paris • Madrid
Capetown • Sydney • Tokyo • Singapore • Mexico City

The publisher offers excellent discounts on this book when ordered in quantity for bulk purchases or special sales, which may include electronic versions and/or custom covers and content particular to your business, training goals, marketing focus, and branding interests. For more information, please contact:

U.S. Corporate and Government Sales
(800) 382-3419
corpsales@pearsontechgroup.com

For sales outside the United States, please contact:

International Sales
international@pearsoned.com

Visit us on the Web: informit.com/aw

Library of Congress Cataloging-in-Publication Data

Brown, Paul C.
  Architecting complex-event processing solutions with TIBCO / Paul C. Brown.
    pages cm
  Includes index.
  ISBN 978-0-321-80198-2 (pbk. : alk. paper) — ISBN 0-321-80198-9 (pbk. : alk. paper)
1. Business logistics—Data processing. 2. Event processing (Computer science)
3. TIBCO Software Inc. I. Title.
  HD38.5.B76 2014
  658.50285'53—dc23   2013026369

ISBN-13: 978-0-321-80198-2
ISBN-10:   0-321-80198-9

Text printed in the United States on recycled paper at RR Donnelley in Crawfordsville, Indiana.
First printing, September 2013

To Mugs and Willie

Contents

Preface

Complex-Event Processing

Complex-event processing is a nontraditional style of building solutions. This style makes it possible to address problems that do not yield well to traditional approaches such as real-time situation analysis. More broadly, complex-event processing enables the enterprise to sense, analyze, and respond to its business situations in new and innovative ways—ways that provide extreme value and competitive advantage.

In complex-event processing solutions, the word *complex* comes into play in two very different ways. The first refers to sensing, analyzing, and responding to what is going on. It's not just, "Oh, this event occurred, therefore I need to do <some activity>." It's more complex than that: It requires correlating that event with other events and with contextual information in order to understand whether a situation of business importance exists, and then deciding what, if anything, needs to be done. Complexity in sensing, complexity in analyzing, complexity in responding.

The other way that complexity applies is that complex-event processing involves a wide variety of computational techniques. There is no single approach to sensing, analyzing, and responding that is suitable for all types of situations. Each of the approaches has its own strengths and weaknesses, all of which need to be understood in order for you to craft your solution.

About This Book

This book provides an introduction to the complex-event processing space and the computational approaches enabled by TIBCO BusinessEvents®. It is divided into four parts: Getting Started, Technology, Design Patterns, and Deployment.

Part I, Getting Started, provides a conceptual overview of the complex-event processing space. It discusses how complex-event processing can be employed in a business context to provide competitive differentiation, covers the terminology of complex-event processing, and explores the ways in which complex-event processing is different from traditional computing. It also explores a number of business applications for complex-event processing.

Part II, Technology, covers the capabilities of the TIBCO Business Events® product suite. It covers the TIBCO Business Events suite of products and presents a life-cycle overview of solutions based on these products. The TIBCO Business Events executable, a Java virtual machine (JVM), can be configured with combinations of five functional components: inference agents, cache agents, query agents, process agents, and dashboard agents. Inference agents process rules, and cache agents provide the information-sharing mechanism within TIBCO BusinessEvents. Query agents provide both snapshot and continuous queries of cached information. Process agents provide orchestration capabilities, while dashboard agents provide real-time visualization capabilities. The architecture and functionality of each type of agent are explored.

Part III, Design Patterns, explores the building-block design patterns used in constructing complex-event processing solutions with TIBCO BusinessEvents. Patterns for recognizing situation changes, comparisons and changes to reference data, systems of record, handling duplicate inputs, run-time rule changes, and orchestrating actions are explored. Patterns for pattern recognition, integration, solution modularization, information sharing, locking, load distribution, and sequencing are covered.

Part IV, Deployment, covers the architecturally significant aspects of putting a solution into production. The Nouveau Health Care case study is a realistic design problem that illustrates many of the issues an architect needs to address. It is used as an example to explore performance, modularization for deployment, managing the cache and backing store, defining deployment patterns, and monitoring. Design patterns for solution fault tolerance, high availability, and site disaster recovery are discussed, along with best practices for the conduct of complex-event processing projects.

The organization of the book is shown in Figure P-1.

Online Examples

Many of the examples in this book are taken from actual TIBCO BusinessEvents projects that are available online. All of these projects begin with the prefix ACEPST and can be found at informit.com/title/9780321801982.

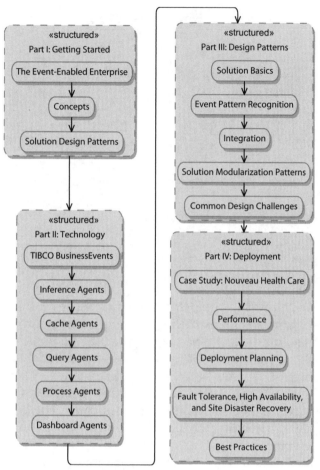

Figure P-1: *Organization of the Book*

TIBCO Architecture Book Series

Architecting Complex-Event Processing Solutions with TIBCO® is the third book in a series on architecting solutions with TIBCO products (Figure P-2). It builds upon the material covered in *TIBCO® Architecture Fundamentals,* which provides material common to all TIBCO-based designs. Each of the more advanced books, including this one, explores a different style of solution, all based on TIBCO technology. Each explores the additional TIBCO products that are relevant to that style of solution. Each defines larger and more specialized architecture patterns relevant to the style, all built on top of the foundational set of design patterns presented in *TIBCO® Architecture Fundamentals.*

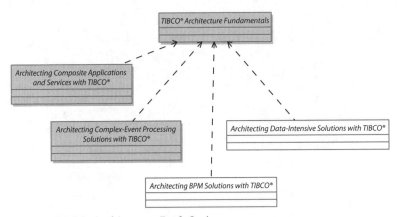

Figure P-2: *TIBCO Architecture Book Series*

Intended Audience

Project architects are the intended primary audience for this book. These are the individuals responsible for defining an overall complex-event processing solution and specifying the components and services required to support that solution. Experienced architects will find much of interest, but no specific prior knowledge of architecture is assumed in the writing. This is to ensure that the material is also accessible to novice architects and advanced designers. For this latter audience, however, a reading of *TIBCO® Architecture Fundamentals*[1] and *Architecting Composite Applications and Services with TIBCO®*[2] is highly recommended. These books explore integration and services along with the broader topics of solution architecture specification and documentation.

TIBCO specialists in a complex-event processing center of excellence will find material of interest, including background on TIBCO BusinessEvents product suite and related best-practice design patterns. The material on performance and tuning lays the foundation for building high-performance applications based on the product suite.

1. Paul C. Brown, *TIBCO® Architecture Fundamentals*, Boston: Addison-Wesley (2011).

2. Paul C. Brown, *Architecting Composite Applications and Services with TIBCO®*, Boston: Addison-Wesley (2013).

Enterprise architects will find content of interest as well. The collection of design patterns, in conjunction with those presented in *TIBCO®* *Architecture Fundamentals*, provides the basis for a baseline set of standard design patterns for the enterprise.

Detailed Learning Objectives

After reading this book, you will be able to

- Describe the characteristics of an event-enabled enterprise
- Explain the concepts related to complex-event processing
- List examples of complex-event processing solutions
- Describe the TIBCO BusinessEvents product suite
- Explain the operation and tuning of TIBCO BusinessEvents agents
- Explain how situations and changes in situations can be recognized
- Describe how rules can be changed at runtime
- Explain how activities can be orchestrated
- Describe how patterns of events can be recognized
- Modularize complex-event processing solutions to facilitate maintainability and scalability
- Describe how to share information among distributed components of a complex-event processing solution
- Select and apply appropriate patterns for load distribution, fault tolerance, high availability, and site disaster recovery
- Explain how design choices impact agent performance
- Define deployment patterns for complex-event processing solutions
- Describe the best practices for conducting complex-event processing projects

Acknowledgments

I must begin by acknowledging the extraordinary contribution of Rodrigo Abreu in formulating the content of this book and the accompanying TIBCO Education course. Not only was he instrumental in helping me fine-tune the scope of material to be covered, but he also clarified (often by experiment) many questions about actual product behavior. This was all in addition to his "day job," and often on his own time. It is fair to say that without his assistance, neither this book nor the accompanying course would exist. I am in his debt.

This book and accompanying course started out as a conversation with Paul Vincent in September 2010. The outline we put together at that time has stood the test of time and it can still be clearly recognized in the finished product. Wenyan Ma made many valuable contributions in defining the scope of material to be covered, and Michael Roeschter made significant contributions to the content.

Many others have contributed to the technical content: Pranab Dhar, Sergio Gonik, Ryan Hollom, Fatih Ildiz, Ali Nikkhah, Mitul Patel, Nicolas Prade, Patrick Sapinski, Rajarsi Sarkar, Rajesh Senapathy, Piotr Smolinski, Suresh Subramani, Piotr Szuszkiewicz, and Yueming Xu. I am grateful for their contributions.

My deepest thanks to the TIBCO Education team who worked with me on this project: Alan Brown, Mike Fallon, Michelle Jackson, and Madan Mashalkar. In more ways than I can mention, they made it all happen. Special thanks to Jan Plutzer, who strongly supported this effort from its inception.

Without the strong support of Eugene Coleman, Paul Asmar, and Murat Sonmez, I would not have been able to dedicate the time necessary for this effort. You have my deepest gratitude.

I would like to acknowledge those who took the time to review the manuscript: Abby Brown, Antonio Bruno, Benjamin Dorman, Jose Estefania, Lloyd Fischer, Alexandre Jeong, James Keegan, Lee Kleir, Edward Rayl, Michael Roeschter, and Mark Shelton. Your feedback has significantly improved the book.

I would like to thank the folks at Addison-Wesley for their continued support. Peter Gordon, my editor, has been a thoughtful guide through five books. Kim Boedigheimer continues to work behind-the-scenes magic to make things happen. The production team—Julie Nahil, Megan Guiney, and Diane Freed—did their usual fine work in making this book a reality.

Finally, I would like to thank my wife, Maria, and my children, Jessica and Philip, for their love and support.

About the Author

Dr. Paul C. Brown is a Principal Software Architect at TIBCO Software Inc. His work centers on enterprise and large-scale solution architectures, the roles of architects, and the organizational and management issues surrounding these roles. His total architecture approach, the concurrent design of both business processes and information systems, can reduce project duration by 25 percent. He has architected tools for designing distributed control systems, process control interfaces, internal combustion engines, and NASA satellite missions. Dr. Brown is the author of *Succeeding with SOA: Realizing Business Value Through Total Architecture* (2007), *Implementing SOA: Total Architecture In Practice* (2008), *TIBCO® Architecture Fundamentals* (2011), *Architecting Composite Applications and Services with TIBCO®* (2012), and *Architecting Complex-Event Processing Solutions with TIBCO®* (2014), all from Addison-Wesley, and he is a coauthor of the *SOA Manifesto* (soamanifesto.org). He received his Ph.D. in computer science from Rensselaer Polytechnic Institute and his BSEE from Union College. He is a member of IEEE and ACM.

Part I

Getting Started

Chapter 1

The Event-Enabled Enterprise

Objectives

The pragmatic question that arises when discussing complex-event processing in a business context is, "Why?" What is it about this approach that makes it interesting as a business investment?

Answering this question is the focus of this chapter. After reading this chapter you will be able to explain the concept of an event-enabled enterprise and describe how such an enterprise gains competitive advantage through innovations in its ability to sense, analyze, and respond to its business environment.

Extreme Value

Enterprises, whether they are commercial companies or governmental agencies, exist to provide value to their constituents. Enterprises that cease to deliver value soon cease to exist. Those that continue to deliver modest value survive. Enterprises that deliver what Vivek Ranadivé refers to as *extreme value* soon outstrip their competition and prosper.

One example of extreme value is the iPhone. When the iPhone was introduced in 2007 it cost substantially more than basic cell phones.

Yet people bought the iPhone—even people who had barely enough money for food. Why? What value did the iPhone offer that was so compelling that people who arguably couldn't afford them still bought them?

The answer is that the iPhone (and other types of smart phone) enables people to interact with the world around them in new and innovative ways. It enables people to sense what is going on, analyze the situation, and respond to the world—and to do so in real time, anywhere they happen to be. The user senses in new ways, no longer just by receiving phone calls but now by receiving text messages, e-mails, social media posts, and alerts from apps as well. The user analyzes what is going on in new ways, not only by using their address book and other personal reference information but also by using web browsers, social media, and apps. The user can respond not only with phone calls but also by using this new technology to communicate with others, purchase products, and make reservations. The iPhone makes it possible for the user to sense, analyze, and respond to the world around them anywhere and anytime they choose. This is the extreme value delivered by the iPhone.

So what makes extreme value important to your enterprise? Extreme value turns customers into fans—fans who prefer the products and services of your enterprise to the exclusion of its competitors. Fans whose attitude is, as the 1960s commercial put it, "I'd rather fight than switch!" (Figure 1-1). Fans whose loyalty to your enterprise fosters its growth and profitability. So how can complex-event processing enable your enterprise to deliver extreme value?

Figure 1-1: *"I'd Rather Fight than Switch!"*

Sense, Analyze, and Respond

What provides the user of the iPhone with extreme value is the ability to innovate, particularly in how the user interacts with the world. Enterprises can benefit by innovating in similar ways—specifically, in how they sense, analyze, and respond to the needs of their customers and business partners.

Enterprises deliver value to their customers through their business processes. If you think about how a business process does this, each process senses something that is going on, analyzes the situation to determine whether action is required and what action to take, and responds by executing those actions. The enterprise senses an order from a business, analyzes the order by validating it and checking the company's credit, and responds by shipping the requested goods and invoicing the business. The enterprise senses a change in stock inventory, analyzes it to determine whether new inventory needs to be ordered, and orders replenishment stock if necessary. Everything the enterprise does is through business processes, and business processes are nothing more than an organized way of sensing, analyzing, and responding to the enterprise's ecosystem.

A significant way in which an enterprise can gain competitive advantage is by improving its business processes. Businesses respond faster, offering next-day or same-day delivery instead of asking customers to wait six to eight weeks. Businesses sense customer needs and provide value-added services. Auto dealerships locate suitable financing for their customers, saving their customers time and trouble. Businesses develop an understanding of customer preferences. Retailers leverage customer loyalty programs to make targeted offers that not only please the customer by only making offers for things they are truly interested in, but also increase the efficiency of the marketing process and thus lowering the cost of sales.

Every business process improvement is a change to the way in which that process senses, analyzes, and responds to the world around it. Sometimes this means doing things faster—doing them now. Sometimes this means doing them better—having the right information at the right time. Sometimes this means doing it cheaper—using more cost-effective resources to get the job done. Gaining competitive advantage—the two-second advantage—requires improving business processes through innovation in sensing, analyzing, and responding.

Innovation in Sensing, Analyzing, and Responding

Pre-computer business processes were driven exclusively by human activity. Each process started when one person took an action: a customer placed an order; an associate recorded the results of an inventory check. Someone else sensed this initial activity: the salesman recorded the order; the store manager received the updated inventory. Someone analyzed what was sensed to determine the appropriate response: the salesman validated the order and the pricing; the store manager determined which items required reordering. Someone responded to this situation: the salesman submitted the order for fulfillment; the store manager ordered replacement inventory.

This sense-analyze-respond pattern is pervasive. Every participant in every business process performs these three functions. The participants interact with each other, each sensing what other participants have done and responding accordingly. When you include information systems as participants in business processes, each system has to sense some activity, analyze what it has sensed, and respond accordingly. The collaboration of these participants, human and system alike, creates an overall business process that, viewed as a whole, defines how the enterprise senses, analyzes, and responds.

When it comes to improving a business process, every improvement to every business process is an improvement in sensing, analyzing, and responding somewhere in that business process. Let's take a look at the types of innovations that can be applied.

Innovation in Sensing

The sensing functionality of many business processes is passive; the process waits for a person or a system to submit a request. The sales process waits for the customer to place an order; the stock replenishment process waits for an associate to update an inventory level.

Active sensing—sensing business significant events—can speed up processes. Consider the case of the stock replenishment process. Instead of manually taking inventory, you might maintain a running inventory that is automatically updated each time an item is sold, and then use this inventory to automatically order replenishment stock. Implementing such an innovation requires changes to three business processes: the Sales Process, the Inventory Management Process, and the Replenishment Process. The Sales Process changes are

- Sensing which products are being sold (e.g., using bar-code scanning)
- Responding by generating point-of-sale transaction records that identify the products and quantities sold

The Inventory Management Process changes are

- Sensing the point-of-sale transactions as they occur
- Analyzing each transaction to determine which product inventories require updating
- Responding by updating the inventory record

The Replenishment Process changes are

- Sensing the change in inventory level
- Analyzing the change to determine whether new stock needs to be ordered
- Responding by ordering new stock as required

Active sensing—automation—requires the sensing of business significant events and the subsequent analysis of and response to those events. In the previous example, there are three significant events: identification of the item being sold, sale of the goods, and updating of the inventory.

Often one of the challenges you will face in active sensing is the lack of an observable event. Prior to bar-code scanning, for example, there really was no identification of what was being sold at the cash register. Only high-value items such as cars and appliances had sales receipts that identified the specific items being sold. Active sensing often requires changes to the process that make the events of interest observable in an automated way.

A key difference between active and passive sensing is timeliness. Passively, the point-of-sale transactions might accumulate in a file or database, and the sensing might be done on a periodic basis by reading those records. Actively, the point-of-sale transactions might be published—announced—as they occur. Subscribers—announcement listeners—are informed immediately when a transaction occurs.

Another key difference is data quality. Passively, during the time between one periodic inventory update and the next, the inventory data is out of date. Actively, the inventory data is up to date within seconds of the actual transaction—before the goods have even left the store. Errors in data can result in faulty decisions that adversely impact the enterprise.

In summary, there are two possible innovations in sensing. One is automating the sensing of business-significant events and thus providing information about what has occurred. The other is propagating those events in real time, as they are happening, and thus facilitating timely responses and improving data quality.

Innovation in Analysis

Once an event of business significance has been sensed, some evaluation may be required to determine what, if anything, needs to be done. Such analysis typically requires access to reference information, which raises two questions: How is the reference information accessed, and when does the analysis occur? Both provide opportunities for innovation.

Reference information often needs to be retrieved. If the same reference information needs to be retrieved repeatedly, accessing it can be computationally expensive. One approach to dealing with this is to accumulate the sensed events and perform the analysis periodically on batches of events. Such batching leads to delays in analysis and the subsequent responses.

An alternative approach is to stage the reference information in such a way that the analysis of the event can occur immediately without a significant computational penalty. This makes possible the immediate analysis of events as they occur, making possible immediate responses as well.

If events are analyzed soon enough, it then becomes possible to recognize an emerging situation before it actually occurs. This is what Vivek Ranadivé refers to as the two-second advantage.[1] This anticipation makes it possible to take action and either take advantage of the situation or alter the outcome. For example, a bank might observe one of its good customers using its web site mortgage calculator and proactively make an offer for a mortgage to that customer.

In summary, there are two possible innovations in analysis. One is positioning reference information so that its retrieval does not present a computational barrier to analysis. The other is to perform the analysis in real time, as the events occur. Doing both of these makes it possible to anticipate situations before they occur and leverage that anticipation through appropriate actions.

---

1. Vivek Ranadivé and Kevin Maney, *The Two-Second Advantage: How We Succeed by Anticipating the Future—Just Enough*, London: Hodder & Stoughton (2011).

Innovation in Response

Analyzing events results in an understanding that a particular situation exists and a determination of what type of response, if any, is required. Innovation in response lies in improving the interaction between the party performing the analysis and the party executing the action. In all cases, requests (which are simply another form of event) must be sent to the party doing the work. However, there are two choices that impact the timeliness of the work performance. One choice lies in the delivery of the requests: Requests may be sent immediately, or they may accumulate and be sent periodically. The other choice lies in the timeliness of work performance: Work may be performed immediately upon request, or it may be performed at some later time.

Delays in work performance can negate any advantage gained in anticipating a situation. This is not to say that all work must be performed immediately, but rather that the timing of the work performance must be appropriate for the present situation.

In summary, there are two possible innovations in response. One is sending work requests immediately as soon as the need for the work is recognized. The other is in performing the work either immediately or within a timeframe appropriate to take advantage of a recognized situation. Together, these innovations enable the enterprise to respond more appropriately.

The Event-Enabled Enterprise

From a business perspective, innovations in sensing, analyzing, and responding enable the enterprise to not only react faster and more appropriately to situations, but also to be proactive, anticipating situations and taking advantage of that anticipation. Both enable the enterprise to increase the value they deliver to their customers and business partners and gain competitive advantage. Realizing this business value requires the automation of sense, analysis, and response activities along with the appropriate positioning of reference information for immediate and efficient use.

So what is an event-enabled enterprise? It is simply an enterprise that has the infrastructure in place to sense, analyze, and respond to events as they occur and has positioned reference information to support this real-time activity. The event-enabled enterprise is thus in a position to efficiently innovate in how it senses, analyzes, and responds to the world around it. Through continuous innovation in these areas, the event-enabled enterprise distinguishes itself from its competitors and builds competitive advantage. Done well, such innovations provide extreme value for its customers, turning them into loyal fans.

Summary

Extreme value sets your enterprise apart from its peers and turns your customers into loyal fans. Business process improvements are one way of providing this extreme value. These improvements make your enterprise more responsive to its customer base by innovations in how the enterprise senses, analyzes, and responds to the world around it. The most significant innovation lies in performing these activities in real time. Proactively sensing events—recognizing that something has happened rather than passively waiting to be told—is a significant enabler for this type of process improvement. The event-enabled enterprise is one that recognizes such events and continuously innovates in its analysis and response. It delivers extreme value to its customers.

Chapter 2

Concepts

Objectives

The event-enabled enterprise concept is, itself, build upon a number of ideas. As a prerequisite to having a meaningful discussion about realizing the event-enabled enterprise, these underlying concepts must first be clearly understood. That is the purpose of this chapter.

After reading this chapter you will understand the essential concepts underlying the event-enabled enterprise: events, complex events, complex-event processing, context, event responses, and event-driven processes.

Overview

The event-enabled enterprise (Figure 2-1) innovates in the manner in which it senses, analyzes, and responds to the world around it. It senses events that are happening in the world. When it senses an event occurring outside the enterprise, it announces the fact within the enterprise. This announcement becomes an internal event within the enterprise. The announcement triggers an analysis of the event, determining its business significance and whether a business response is required. The announcement that a response is required is another event, one that triggers the actual response. The response is an action, and the

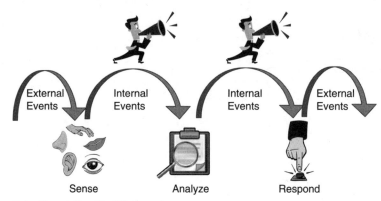

Figure 2-1: *Event-Enabled Enterprise*

completion of this action is, itself, an event—one that may be observable outside the enterprise. This is the way an event-enabled enterprise works.

Events

An event is simply something that occurs: an order is placed, a service is delivered, a customer arrives on premises. To act on the event, you need to know what occurred and perhaps when it occurred, but first and foremost you need to recognize that it happened. The question is, how?

Recognizing Events

On the surface, recognizing an event may appear trivial: The customer placed an order. But dig a bit deeper and some challenges appear. What if you are using a commercial off-the-shelf (COTS) software package to manage your orders? The event you seek is internal to the software package, an update to the database that underlies the system. What if the system does not provide a mechanism—a callback—to inform other components that an order has been placed?

In cases like this you must identify a mechanism for recognizing such events. There are a number of standard techniques for doing this. These techniques and their implementations are discussed in the companion book *TIBCO® Architecture Fundamentals.*[1]

---

1. Paul C. Brown, *TIBCO® Architecture Fundamentals*, Boston: Addison-Wesley (2011).

Sometimes there is an existing artifact whose creation signifies the event you are looking for: a file that is generated or a message that is sent. In such cases the recognition of the event can be accomplished by capturing of a copy of the artifact. *TIBCO® Architecture Fundamentals* also covers techniques for doing this.

The most challenging situations are those in which there is nothing on a technical level to observe. The Telecommunications Restoration of Service case study (see sidebar) discusses a business case in which this situation arose. In such cases, there is always some IT work involved, and possibly some changes in business practices as well, just to be able to recognize the occurrence of events.

Case Study: Telecommunications Restoration of Service

As part of its services agreement, a telecommunications company has established a service-level agreement (SLA) that stipulates the maximum time it will take to restore service in the event of an outage. The service-level agreement establishes a financial penalty that will be incurred should service not be restored within this period of time.

In practice, customers are calling and complaining that the SLA is not being met and claiming the related financial penalties. The telecommunications company is not aware that the SLAs are being violated: its monitoring of the service restoration process is inadequate.

As a result of this situation, the telecommunications company tries to implement a monitor for the outage recovery process. This monitor contains a model of what is supposed to be happening. Tracking the actual process requires capturing the events that show what is actually happening: poles being planted, wires being strung, and so forth.

In implementing the monitor, the company encounters a problem: Many of the events that mark what is happening are simply not observable. Much of the service restoration work is outsourced to subcontractors who plant poles and string wires. The contracts with these subcontractors specify how the work requests will be exchanged and how the completion of the work will be reported (often long after the fact), but they do not make any provisions at all for reporting intermediate status.

Because of this situation, the company has no choice other than to implement the monitor in multiple phases. In the first phase, a limited process monitor is implemented using the events that are presently observable. In parallel, the company embarks on a renegotiation of the contracts, adding intermediate reporting requirements for the subcontractors and specifying the mechanisms to be used for this reporting. It initiates an IT project to add the interfaces required for the reporting of the events. Finally, it upgrades the monitoring to take advantage of the newly observable events. The eventual cost savings from improving the management of the service restoration process more than covers the cost of this work.

Simple Event Recognition May Be Inadequate

Sometimes the business significant situation you are trying to recognize doesn't correspond to a single event that can be observed. If you are looking for potential fraud on an account, a single failed login may not be significant: Users frequently make mistakes entering their userids and passwords. What is significant is that there have been repeated failed login attempts within a short period of time: for example, three failed logins in five minutes. In order to recognize the business-significant situation, the present event (the latest failed login attempt) must be correlated with earlier failed-login events. Events that require some kind of analysis in order to recognize an event of business significance are called complex events, a topic that will be discussed in more detail shortly.

Categories of Events

Events can be categorized in a number of ways. These categorizations often impact the approach you will use to sense, analyze, and respond to the events, so these must be kept in mind as you conceptualize your solutions.

Technical and Business Events

Events that can be directly observed are called *technical events*. Typically what is detected is a state change (e.g., a database update) in an application or a communication between components. *Business events* represent occurrences that are of business significance. But there is not always a 1:1 correspondence between technical and business events.

Some technical events represent occurrences that are of business significance, others (in fact, the majority of technical events) do not. Every click on every link on a website and every message being sent between systems is an occurrence that can be observed. However, only a subset of these technical events will likely be of business significance.

Simple and Complex Events

A *simple event* is a business event that is also a technical event. But some business events don't correspond to a single technical event: Their recognition is the result of an analysis that determines something of business significance has occurred. Events that require this type of analysis are referred to as *complex events*.

Point and Interval Events

Usually when you think about an event you associate the occurrence of the event with a point in time: the time at which the order was submitted or the time that the power failed. Generally, this is the time at which a technical event was captured. Such events are referred to as *point events*.

Some events, however, occur over a period of time. For example, the TIBCO User Conference (TUCON) is an event that takes place over several days. A television show happens over the course of 30 minutes or an hour. Events that occur over some period of time are *interval events*.

Why is this distinction important? It is important when you need to compare the temporal relationships between two events: Comparing interval events is more complicated than comparing point events. For a pair of point events, there are only three possible relationships: before, simultaneous, or after. For interval events, there are fifteen possible relationships between two events (Figure 2-2). The last two relationships are special cases in which one of the events has degenerated into a point event that is coincident with either the start or the end of the remaining interval.

Missing Events

Sometimes the business-relevant event you are looking for is the observance that some other event was not observed, at least when it was expected. These cases arise when there is a service-level agreement regarding when an event should occur and the expected event does not occur within this time interval. Typically the beginning of this time interval coincides with some previous event: The clock marking the deadline for delivering a product starts when the order is placed.

Sometimes the recognition is more complicated: An event is supposed to occur at some regular intervals, and the observance is that the expected events have been absent for some period of time. This is a common approach to liveness testing: A component sends a heartbeat at regular intervals indicating that it is operating properly. The absence of these heartbeats for some period of time is an indication that there is a problem.

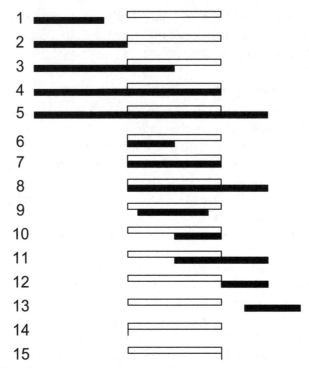

Figure 2-2: *Possible Relationships between Two Intervals*

Note that the event marking the recognition of a missing event is always a complex event: Its generation is the result of an analysis triggered by another event, namely the expiration of a timer. The analysis indicates that the expected event has not occurred and results in the generation of an event marking this recognition.

Complex Events

A complex event is one whose recognition requires analysis (Figure 2-3). The analysis itself is triggered by the arrival of an event that serves as the triggering event for the analysis. The expiration of a timer, for example, might serve as the triggering event for an analysis that determines whether an expected event has actually occurred. The triggering event, which could be either a technical or business event, is an indication that some state of the world has changed and consequently an analysis is warranted.

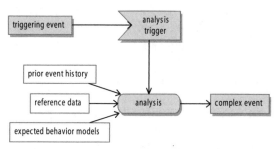

Figure 2-3: *Complex Event*

The complexity and nature of the required analysis varies greatly. Sometimes the analysis is simple: It just examines the current event to determine its business significance. For example, the current event might be a banking transaction, and the analysis determines whether the transaction amount exceeds $10,000 and therefore requires the filing of a Currency Transaction Report with the Internal Revenue Service.[2] Sometimes the analysis is complex, determining whether a pattern indicating fraud has been recognized or whether a process is executing as it should. There are, in fact, many types of analysis that could be performed, each appropriate for recognizing a different kind of situation. In fact, it is the variety of possible types of analysis that lead to the varied feature set of TIBCO BusinessEvents®.

Complex-Event Processing (CEP)

Complex-event processing is a term used to describe the computational activity that is driven by events. The analysis leading up to the recognition of a complex event is one example of complex-event processing. The orchestration of actions taken subsequent to event recognition also falls into this category.

Complex-event processing is challenging for several reasons. One is the rate at which events can occur. Twitter processes hundreds of millions of messages per day, which poses challenges for applications trying to track the nature of the dialogs on Twitter. During peak periods, Visa processes upwards of 20,000 transactions

---

2. In the United States, the Bank Secrecy Act requires banks and thrift institutions to file this report.

per second, posing challenges in identifying patterns indicating fraudulent activity. As the event arrival rate increases, the efficiency with which the event analysis can be performed becomes increasingly important.

Another challenge of CEP is the efficiency with which prior event history, reference data, and expected-behavior models can be accessed and utilized. At 20,000 transactions per second, even the lookup to see whether a credit card number is valid had better be pretty efficient. The more complex the analysis, the more important this becomes.

A third challenge lies in defining the analysis that needs to be performed in response to the arrival of an event. Traditional programming is done procedurally, but the use of rule-based approaches and analytical techniques for recognizing behavior patterns is often more appropriate for the kinds of problems to which complex-event processing is applied. There are many ways in which the analysis can be performed, and selecting the appropriate approach is one of the fundamental complex-event-processing design decisions for each solution.

Let's take a look at a simple example drawn from the banking industry. A common pattern that identifies possible credit-card fraud is a low-value transaction (for example, buying a candy bar for a dollar) followed within a short period of time by a very large purchase ($10,000 worth of stereo equipment). The small transaction is simply to test whether the credit card is working, and then the card is used in earnest.

Based on this example, you might define the following rule for identifying potential fraud:

If there is a very small purchase (<= $5) followed within an hour by a very large purchase (>= $10,000), then generate an event to indicate possible fraud on the account.

A procedural approach to implementing this rule using traditional programming and database techniques is shown in Figure 2-4. If the transaction is less than the large threshold ($10,000), the transaction is simply recorded. When a large transaction comes in, then the previous transactions are queried to determine whether there has been a small transaction within the past hour.

Given that the peak transaction rate might exceed 20,000 transactions per second, it is clear that the efficiency with which the transactions can

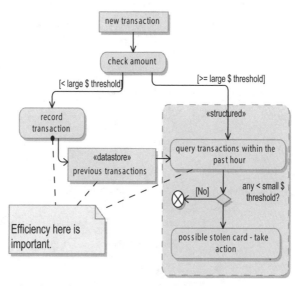

Figure 2-4: *Procedural Analysis*

be recorded and queried is a major issue. This is particularly the case if conventional relational database technology is used for the datastore.

An alternative, rule-based approach is shown in Figure 2-5. New transactions that arrive are placed in memory, and only the last hour's transactions are kept in memory. The arrival of a transaction then triggers a rule. The rule checks to see whether the new transaction exceeds the $10,000 threshold. It then checks to see whether there is another transaction in memory with the same account number, with an amount less than the $5 threshold, and that occurred before the new transaction.

There is more going on here than just the use of a rule for the evaluation: Data is being held in memory, not on disk. The policy for retaining the data in memory is to only hold the past hour's worth of data; the trigger for evaluating the rule is a change to the data in memory. Performing complex-event processing at high rates requires these kinds of specializations in the manner in which data is stored, shared, and analyzed. Complicating things even more, there is no single specialization that is suitable in all circumstances. A major focus of this book is the exploration of various types of computational specializations, with particular emphasis on how they are supported by TIBCO Business Events.

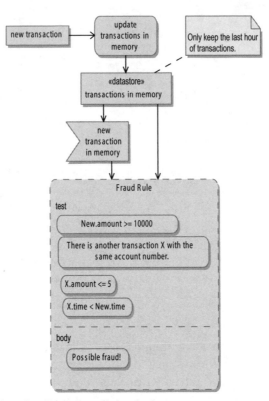

Figure 2-5: *Declarative (Rule-Based) Analysis*

Event Correlation

Individual events typically do not contain all of the information necessary to support an analysis to determine their business relevance.
Correlation of the events with other events, reference data, and behav-
ioral models is required for a richer understanding of those events.

Correlation must be based on some criteria, such as the type of the
event, the time at which the event occurred, or a key identifier such as
an account number, customer ID, or order ID. A new order event might
be correlated with other new order events that have occurred within
the past hour to derive an understanding of how fast orders are being
placed. The derived order rate might indicate how well a particular
social-networking marketing campaign is working. Events can be
correlated with other events based on common information in the
events: product ID, order ID, or customer ID. If a marketing campaign
is focused on specific products, you might want to correlate sales events
with the identifiers of the products targeted by the campaign.

Correlating events with reference data can provide a broader analysis perspective. Using the account number from an event to access other information about the account or using the customer ID to access information about the customer permits this related information to be used as part of the analysis.

Perhaps the richest form of correlation is between an event and a model of the behavior that is expected to be observed. A model of the proper execution of a business process that identifies the events that should be observed during its execution provides an excellent reference for interpreting the events that actually occur. This perspective makes it possible to determine whether the process is executing as planned.

Analysis often combines multiple types of correlation. For example, you might want to analyze the calls coming in to a customer support center to identify customers that are having an unusually hard time getting a problem resolved. Given an initial event indicating an incoming call, you might correlate the telephone number in the event with customer records to identify the customer who is calling. You might also correlate this event with other incoming call events to see whether there were other calls from the same customer within the past hour. If you find three or more events correlated in this way, you might conclude that the customer is having a significant problem and take action by escalating the call to a supervisor. Note that by correlating each call with a customer, you set the stage for recognizing and correlating other calls from that same customer that happen to have originated from different phones (for example, home, mobile, work).

Correlation is fundamental to CEP analysis. As such, when you undertake a CEP project it is prudent to focus your initial attention on identifying the things that need to be correlated and the basis upon which they will be correlated. This understanding will then guide the design of your data structures and inform the rest of your design.

Context

The analysis of an event always requires some form of contextual information. The previous examples involved context, such as reference data and expected-behavior models. In general, context falls into three broad categories:

1. Constants
2. Data
3. Metadata

Constants

Constants are typically used as thresholds for making decisions. The $5 and $10,000 dollar values used earlier are typical examples. Values that are used as thresholds for decisions are often somewhat arbitrary and may be subject to change as conditions vary and understanding evolves. It is thus important to identify whether the values might, in fact, change over time.

Your understanding of whether values are subject to change will alter your design thinking. You can bake constants into the design, but if you do so the only way to subsequently change them is to modify and redeploy the design. It's an IT project.

A more flexible approach is to design your solution in such a way that the values can be changed at runtime without modifying the design. This might involve values that are looked up (and possibly cached) at the time they are used. To address this type of requirement, TIBCO BusinessEvents has a special construct, a rule template, that enables reference values to be modified at runtime. Whatever approach you choose, if values are subject to change it is prudent to design in the change mechanism.

Data

The most common type of context is data. There is a lot of data in use in the enterprise that can be used to support analysis. Some of this is relatively static reference data: customer data, product data, partner data, and so on. Other data is dynamically changing transactional data: orders, shipments, inventory, and so on.

Whether it is reference data or transactional data, you have to consider where the data is coming from, how you are going to gain access to it, and how you are going to stage the data for efficient use in analysis. Efficiency often requires that copies of the data be cached for convenient access, but, of course, the accuracy and consistency of the cache then come into play.

Another form of data that is often required is a recent history of events, either the events themselves or summaries of information about those events. For example, the number of transactions that have occurred in the past hour or the dollar volume of those transactions may be of interest in interpreting current events.

Metadata

Metadata is information about data. A common form of metadata you are probably familiar with is a schema: information about the structure of data. In complex-event processing, other forms of metadata come into play.

One useful form of metadata in CEP is the structure of a data query. The query specifies how to identify a set of data relevant to the current analysis. The metadata of the query (i.e., the definition of the query) can be encoded directly into the analysis logic at design time, but this requires that you be able to formulate the query in advance. There may be times when the query cannot be formulated in advance: The information needed to define the query will not be available until runtime, either because of dynamic changes in business logic or because the query is based on current information. TIBCO BusinessEvents supports both approaches, allowing queries to be defined both at design time and at runtime. These approaches are discussed in Chapter 7.

Another type of CEP metadata is the description of expected behavior, expressed as an expected pattern of events. This pattern description then provides the context for recognizing the pattern as it occurs, or fails to occur. As with queries, some patterns can be defined at design time, while others cannot be defined until runtime. Chapter 11 shows how TIBCO BusinessEvents supports both approaches.

Yet another form of CEP metadata is a process description. TIBCO BusinessEvents has two different metamodels for describing processes. State models, described in Chapter 5, are well suited to monitoring unmanaged processes and determining whether they are executing properly. Business Process Modeling Notation (BPMN) models, described in Chapter 8, are well suited for orchestrating (managing) process execution.

Analysis Requires Context

It should be obvious by now that there is no analysis without appropriate contextual information. The type of contextual information may vary, from constants to data to metadata, but context provides the basis for analysis. Making sure that the required contextual information is readily available for an efficient analysis is a major requirement for every CEP solution architecture.

It is not uncommon for the same event to be analyzed for different purposes. For example, a phone call from a customer to a magazine publisher may be of interest to the customer service department, but it may be of interest to the marketing department as well. Each of these purposes may require different contextual information to support the associated analysis (Figure 2-6). While both departments need to understand who the customer is (assuming it is a customer), the call center is interested in knowing whether there were any prior calls from this customer, who handled them, and to whom they were forwarded. The marketing department, on the other hand, is interested in knowing whether any of the customer's subscriptions are about to expire so that it can take advantage of this opportunity to offer a subscription renewal.

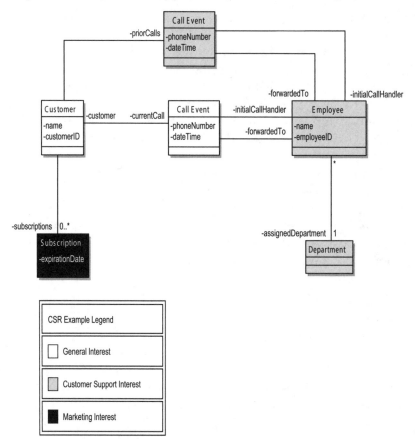

Figure 2-6: *Contextual Information for a Call Event to a Magazine Publisher*

Selecting an Analytical Approach

The discussion up to this point has addressed various aspects of analysis: whether the analysis is defined procedurally or declaratively, and what kind of contextual information might be required. But the core question has yet to be addressed: What conclusions need to be drawn in the analysis, and what is the appropriate approach for drawing those conclusions? These are the central questions underlying every CEP-based solution.

Some analyses are simple. If you want to know whether a service-level agreement has been violated, compare the time it took to actually perform the task to the SLA target for the task. This is simple threshold detection—compare a varying value against a benchmark to determine whether it exceeds the threshold.

Other analyses require more data acquisition and computation. Recognizing that the person using the bank site's mortgage calculator is a customer and has an excellent credit rating takes a bit more doing. Further correlating this recognition with the fact that the bank is actively promoting new mortgage loans and then acting on this correlation to present an offer to the customer while they happen to be present online requires still more design.

CEP analyses can be far more complex than this, so much so that they sometimes even raise feasibility questions. If you can't clearly state the conclusion you are trying to draw and articulate the approach to drawing the conclusion, you are treading on thin ice. For example, the general problem of detecting all possible types of fraud on bank accounts is impossible to solve: The problem itself is not even well defined. It's not clear that you can even articulate all the forms of fraud, let alone identify all the ways in which fraud can be committed. It's an open-ended problem: Criminals are always figuring out new ways to defeat the system and commit fraud. Detecting all possible forms of fraud on bank accounts is not a realistic goal for an IT project.

However, this does not imply that fraud—some specific kinds of fraud—cannot be detected. Far from it. There are many patterns of activity that are significant indicators of possible fraud. Two have already been discussed: multiple failed login attempts in a short period of time and very small transactions followed by very large transactions in a short period of time.

The point is that every project must clearly identify its analytical goals—the conclusions the CEP solution will be required to draw—and identify the techniques that will be used to draw those conclusions.

This should be done before any significant development effort is undertaken. Otherwise, the project will be burdened with repeated rework as half-baked ideas are implemented, found to fail, and discarded.

This is not to say that you should not undertake projects for which the analytical goals and techniques are not yet well defined. The admonition is that if you are undertaking such an effort, you should plan to spend some quality time defining analytical conclusions, developing analytical techniques to draw those conclusions, and validating that the conclusions you have identified accurately identify the actual situation you seek to recognize.

The bottom line is that your first task in a CEP project should be to determine whether you are working on a class of problem for which there are already well-defined analytical techniques. If so, once you educate yourself on these techniques your project will be a straightforward engineering exercise. If not, you need to be realistic and recognize that there is conceptual work (and likely some experimentation) to be done before the engineering task of building a system can begin. You may even need to adjust the project goals to reflect what can reasonably be accomplished within the project's cost and schedule guidelines.

Responding to Events

In most cases the system you are designing needs to do more than simply recognize a situation: It needs to take (or at least initiate) appropriate responses. Determining the appropriate response once the "Ah ha!" moment of situation recognition has occurred can range from simple to complex.

When the event you are responding to is a complex event, one that requires significant analysis, it is good practice to separate the event recognition analysis from the response logic, connecting the two with a new event that announces the situation that has been recognized (Figure 2-7). From a software engineering perspective, this separation of concerns is good practice. Furthermore, the publication of the event announcing the situation allows other responses to be added later without altering the existing design. It adds flexibility.

Figure 2-7: *Responding to Complex Events*

Event responses are generally determined by business rules. Sometimes the rules are not obvious because they are embedded in established practices. In such cases some effort will be required to understand and extract the business rules in preparation for re-implementing them as part of your solution. In other cases the business rules may be codified in well-defined formulas, decision trees, or decision tables ready for incorporation into the solution.

An event response in a CEP solution has a structure similar to that of an event analysis (Figure 2-8). The arrival of an event indicating that some situation exists (which could be either simple or complex) triggers an analysis to determine what the appropriate response should be for this situation. That analysis generally requires some contextual information. The results of the analysis are the events that trigger actions—the enterprise responses to the triggering event.

A trivial example is a business rule that says if the order amount exceeds $500, then an approval is required. The triggering event is the arrival of the order. The analysis is simply a comparison of the order amount with the threshold value. Depending upon your design decisions, the threshold value itself may be fixed in the analysis logic or it may be a piece of contextual information. The action is to initiate the approval process if required.

Trivial as this example is, it does raise an interesting design question with respect to the approval: To what extent should the component doing the response analysis also be responsible for ensuring that the follow-on approval activity is performed? Deciding which component is responsible is an important question for the solution as a whole, as the answer will impact the robustness of the solution.[3]

A richer example is a business rule stating that unless 99% of the received data is valid, the data should be rejected. Here the triggering event is the arrival of the data. However, validating the data will likely

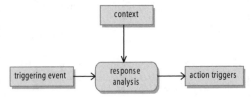

Figure 2-8: *Event Response*

---

3. For an in-depth discussion of the design pattern choices and their impact on the overall solution robustness, see *TIBCO® Architecture Fundamentals.*

require a lot of contextual information and a detailed statement of the validation rules. Even the response rules may be complicated. If the data does not meet the criteria, then clearly the data should be rejected; but if the data does meet the criteria, then the normal processing should be initiated. Again, the question of the CEP component's role in monitoring this subsequent processing must be considered.

In the previous discussion, the tacit assumption has been that the information necessary to perform the validation is simply present as part of the context. But what if validation involves the invocation of services that perform some parts of the validation? Now the analysis takes on the flavor of orchestrating the services of other components, at least for part of the validation. The approach for performing this type of orchestration is a bit different and is described in Chapter 8.

Event-Driven Processes

Events, and the ability to trigger activity based on the receipt of an event, make possible the implementation of an event-driven process as opposed to a request-driven process.

In a request-driven process (Figure 2-9), one party (party A in the figure) does two things: (1) recognizes that some condition has occurred,

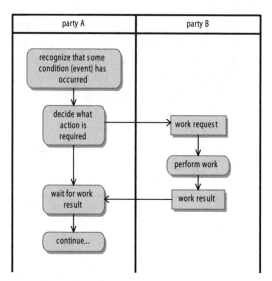

Figure 2-9: *Request-Driven Process*

and (2) decides what action should be taken as a result and then initiates that action.

Figure 2-10 is an example of a request-driven process. Your car breaks. You recognize that it is broken and decide to take the car to the repair shop. You ask the shop to fix your car. The shop diagnoses the problem and determines that your car requires some work for which it needs an authorization. It requests that you authorize the work. Once you have authorized the work, the shop recognizes that it requires parts and requests that the parts provider bring the parts. Once the repair has been completed, the shop requests that you pay for the service. Once you have paid, the repaired car is returned to you. This is the ultimate response to the initial request. This entire process is driven by requests.

In an event-driven process (Figure 2-11), the roles of recognizing a situation and of deciding what action to take are played by different parties. In the figure, party A recognizes that a particular condition

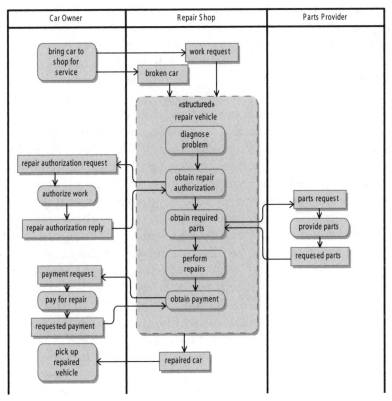

Figure 2-10: *Request-Driven Process Example*

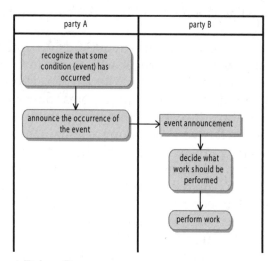

Figure 2-11: *Event-Driven Process*

exists and announces the existence of that condition. The announcement is an event. Party B responds to the event by determining the
action that it considers appropriate and initiating that action.

This separation of responsibilities is the essence of an event-driven
process and gives such processes their unique properties. Because recognition results in an announcement (an event), any party listening to
that announcement can make an independent decision as to what action
to take. This makes it possible to add, remove, or modify individual
action decisions without impacting any of the other components. In
contrast, in a request-driven process one party is making all the action
decisions; any alterations require changes to that component.

Many event-driven processes are augmentations of request-driven
processes. Figure 2-12 shows an event-driven fraud detection process
augmenting a request-driven user login process. The figure shows the
portions of the request-driven process related to the fraud detection.
The hacker submits a login request. After checking to see whether the
account is active (which it will be initially), the web site attempts to
validate the credentials. If the login fails, the failed login screen is displayed and an announcement of the failed login is published. This is
the trigger for the event-driven fraud detection process.

The failed login announcement is added to the record of recent
logins being maintained in memory. The arrival of the new entry triggers an analysis to determine whether there have been three failed
logins in the past five minutes. If so, a security alert (another event) is

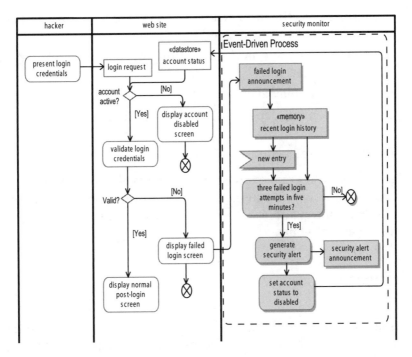

Figure 2-12: *Event-Driven Process Example*

generated, and the account status is set to disabled. This action will impact the subsequent execution of the request-driven process: The next time the hacker tries to log in, the account-disabled screen will be displayed. The hacker won't even get the opportunity to try another userid/password combination.

Of course, there are scenarios that have not been dealt with here that would be required in a real application. These would deal with issues such as re-enabling a user account and updating user credentials.

Event-Enabled Enterprise Capabilities

The concepts discussed in this chapter provide a straightforward way to explain the capabilities of the event-enabled enterprise. The event-enabled enterprise is capable of the following:

- Recognizing and announcing events. This does not necessarily mean that every event is recognized and announced. It means that the enterprise has the infrastructure in place to recognize and raise the visibility of events as needed.

- Immediately analyzing and interpreting events in an appropriate context.
- Recognizing complex events.
- Performing context-dependent analysis to determine appropriate actions.
- Initiating required actions.

These capabilities make it possible for the event-enabled enterprise to innovate in the way it senses, analyzes, and responds to the world around it. Such innovations help it to build competitive advantage and turn customers into fans.

Summary

Events are occurrences, things that happen. Technical events are those that can be directly observed. Business events are those whose recognition has business value. Some business events correspond to a single technical event.

Some events, known as complex events, are the result of an analysis that correlates one or more technical events with contextual information. The analysis determines whether something of business significance has occurred. Different parties may require different contextual information in order to determine the significance of the event.

This type of analysis, involving correlation and reference data, is referred to as complex-event processing. It can be applied both to recognizing situations and to determining appropriate responses.

Contextual information comes in many forms, including constants, reference data, and metadata. One of the significant challenges in complex-event processing is identifying the contextual information that will be required and ensuring its availability to support efficient real-time analysis.

When events drive processes, the result is an event-driven process as opposed to a request-driven process. In a request-driven process a single party both recognizes that a situation has occurred and determines what the response should be. In an event-driven process these two roles are separated, with one party recognizing the situation and announcing it and the other party deciding what action should be taken as a result. This separation leads to architectures that can evolve gracefully.

The event-driven enterprise is one that is able to innovate in the way it senses, analyzes, and responds to the world around it. These innovations can be used to gain competitive advantage.

Chapter 3

CEP Solution Design Patterns

Objectives

There are many different architectural patterns that arise in complex-event processing (CEP) solutions. While all add one or more sense-analyze-respond processes to the enterprise, the manner in which they do so varies widely. This chapter identifies the kinds of variation you can expect and presents a number of well-understood patterns, each of which addresses a common business challenge.

After reading this chapter you will be able to explain the variability in CEP architectures and describe the following patterns:

- Condition Detection
- Situation Recognition
- Track and Trace
- Business Process Timeliness Monitor
- Decision as a Service
- Situational Response
- Orchestrated Response

You will also be able to explain the challenges associated with pioneering projects that develop new solution patterns.

Variability in CEP Architectures

The core CEP process (Figure 3-1) is always the same: Some event is sensed, it is analyzed in the context of some reference data to determine whether something of business interest has occurred, and some decision is made about what the nature of the response ought to be. Yet despite the fact that the core process is always the same, there are many different architectures for complex-event processing. Why?

There are two dominant reasons for the variability in CEP architectures: the handling of reference data and the partitioning of functionality.

Handling Reference Data

The first area of variability centers around the relationship between the reference data and the events being analyzed: Does the stream of events alter the reference data that is used to interpret subsequent events? Applications in which the stream of events does not alter the reference data are relatively straightforward. The primary challenge in these applications is obtaining access to the reference data, which almost always originates elsewhere, and making access to the data efficient during the analysis and response activities.

On the other hand, applications in which the stream of events modifies the reference data are much more complicated. The portion of the reference data that represents the history of prior events does not have a system of record, at least without additional design. If it is unacceptable to lose this historical data when systems are shut down or fail, then the CEP solution must now include a system of record for the historical data. The system of record requires careful and clever design to ensure that it can handle the stream of data changes efficiently and robustly— and still make the data efficiently accessible to the analysis and response activities (Figure 3-2).

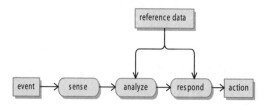

Figure 3-1: *Core CEP Process*

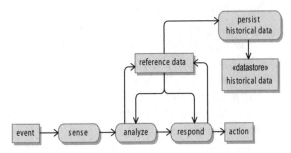

Figure 3-2: *Persisting Historical Data*

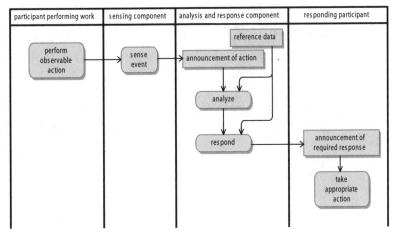

Figure 3-3: *Basic CEP Functional Partitioning*

Partitioning Functionality

The other area of variability lies in the many ways in which the CEP functionality can be partitioned and assigned to different components. The basic partitioning found in CEP solutions is shown in Figure 3-3.

Generally, the events driving the process are the observable actions of a participant (human or system) in some business process. Most of these participants do not announce their activities, at least to components not engaged in that business process. For this reason, CEP solutions generally have one or more components dedicated to sensing these actions and announcing their observations.

The techniques used for these observations are the same ones traditionally used in application integration. These techniques, and the products that support them, are detailed in *TIBCO*™ *Architecture*

Fundamentals.[1] The relevant observation here, however, is that the products used for sensing are, for the most part, not the products used for CEP analysis and response. Thus the participant that does the sensing is generally not the participant doing the analysis and response.

As a side note, one of the hallmarks of the event-enabled enterprise is that its architecture includes the types of components necessary to sense and announce actions and the types of components necessary to analyze and respond to those announcements.

In many cases, the volume of events handled by many CEP solutions makes it impractical to have one component handle all of the events and perform all of the analysis and response processing. Once this point is reached, there are a variety of ways in which performance can be increased. One is to simply deploy multiple instances of the component performing the analysis and response. This is a straightforward approach if the reference data is not updated when events occur. But when the reference data is updated by events, sharing the history across multiple instances of the analysis and response components requires additional design. The design patterns for this are discussed in Chapter 14.

Another approach to scalability is to begin to partition the functionality across additional components. Figure 3-4 shows one possible partitioning in which the analysis that leads up to situation recognition is performed by one component and the determination of the required responses is performed by another. Partitioning patterns also become more complex when the analysis and response computations also

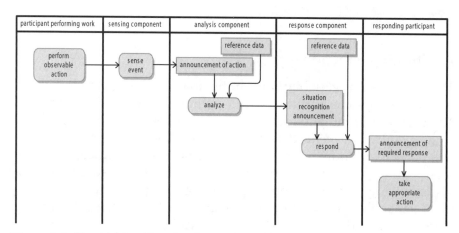

Figure 3-4: *Partitioning Situation Recognition from Response*

---

1. Paul C. Brown, *TIBCO® Architecture Fundamentals*, Boston: Addison-Wesley (2011).

update reference data. Chapter 13 discusses this and other partition-ings as well as the tradeoffs that need to be considered.

As should be obvious by now, there are many possible functional partitionings for CEP solutions. Some lead to simple and straightfor-ward implementations. Others require clear architectural thinking to achieve the desired behavior in a robust and highly scalable fashion.

The following sections discuss a number of CEP solution design pat-terns, each focused on providing a commonly required business capa-bility. For the most part, the patterns are arranged somewhat in order of increasing complexity. The chapter concludes with a brief discussion of problems for which there may not be well-established design patterns.

For simplicity, the sensing component is not shown in these design patterns: It is assumed to be always present.

Condition Detection

The simplest solution pattern you will encounter in complex-event processing is threshold detection (Figure 3-5). In this pattern, a compo-nent takes an action that can be observed and results in a technical event. The condition detector is listening for this event, whose arrival serves as the trigger for analysis. The analysis compares a value con-veyed by the event to a threshold value and, if the event value exceeds the threshold value, generates a business event announcing this condi-tion. Completing the pattern, another component is listening for these announcements and taking appropriate actions.

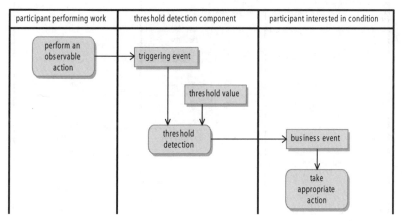

Figure 3-5: *Threshold Detection Pattern*

In using this pattern the location of the threshold value must be considered. One option is to permanently fix the threshold value in the analysis logic. Another option is to make it a piece of contextual information that is looked up by the condition detector, either when it starts or each time an event is analyzed. Yet another option is to use infrastructure that makes it possible to change the value at runtime. TIBCO BusinessEvents® rule templates provide this capability, as described in Chapter 10.

The more general form of this pattern is the Condition Detection pattern (Figure 3-6). In this pattern the detected condition is defined by a number of values that define the boundaries of the condition being recognized. The information considered in the analysis is generally a combination of event and contextual data. If the condition is detected, then a business event is generated announcing the existence of the condition.

When using this pattern the sources of the parameters defining the boundary conditions and the contextual data required to detect the condition must be considered, along with the possible need to change some of these values at runtime. The design effort required to provide access to information originating in other systems and make it efficiently available is often a major part of a CEP project.

In the Condition Detection pattern, the reference data that is used is not modified by the processing of events: It does not reflect prior history. The only state information being used is that conveyed by the

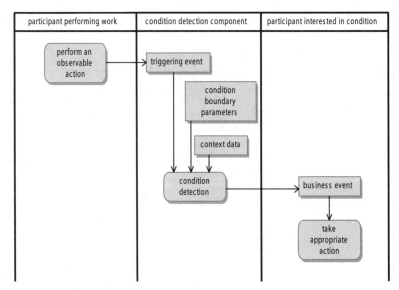

Figure 3-6: *Condition Detection Pattern*

triggering event. This makes the condition detector stateless, and therefore easy to scale and make highly available.

Situation Recognition

The Situation Recognition pattern (Figure 3-7), on the surface, looks a lot like the Condition Detection pattern. However, there is a major difference: In the Situation Recognition pattern, the context data used to recognize a situation when the triggering event arrives contains historical information. Many of the triggering events that arrive do not result in a business event, but their occurrence results in the modification of the context data. The updated context data then provides the context for evaluating the next event that arrives.

Since the context data in this pattern contains historical information, the ability of the pattern to recognize a situation may be compromised if the historical data is lost. Such a loss would occur if the situation recognition component is holding context data in memory and the component is restarted. For this reason, the use of this pattern almost always requires persisting the historical information and recovering this information when the component restarts. The object persistence discussion in Chapter 6 discusses techniques for doing this.

There are many variations on this pattern both in the manner in which the context data keeps track of prior history and the manner in which the historical information is used to interpret a current event. Chapter 10 discusses a number of design patterns that can be used for this purpose.

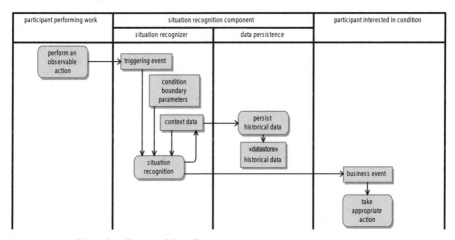

Figure 3-7: *Situation Recognition Pattern*

Track and Trace

The Track-and-Trace pattern (Figure 3-8) is a special case of the Situation Recognition pattern. This pattern involves two contextual elements: a model of the expected process and the state of an existing instance of that process. If the triggering event marks the beginning of a new process execution, an initial process state is created. For other events, information in the event is used to locate the state of the process already being executed (there may be many instances of the process being executed at any given point in time). Once the current state has been identified, the process model is then used to interpret the triggering event in the context of that state.

This simplified example omits a common challenge: the handling of out-of-sequence events. In many real-world situations, events may arrive out of sequence. In some cases, the first event that arrives may not be the initial event in the process. In a full solution, additional logic must be added to handle these situations. Chapter 14 discusses some of the design considerations.

The state machine approach provides for a rich and varied interpretation of the process execution. If the triggering event corresponds to

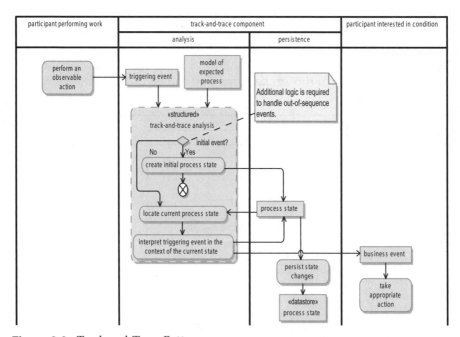

Figure 3-8: *Track-and-Trace Pattern*

an expected transition in the state machine (given the current state), the conclusion is that the process is executing in an expected manner—at least at this time. The analysis can be designed to announce business events when particular states have been achieved (i.e, announce that a milestone has been reached).

If the triggering event does not correspond to an expected transition, something unexpected has happened. Again, the analysis can be designed to emit business events announcing this unexpected situation.

This type of analysis is appropriate for monitoring any type of unmanaged process. Tracking of a package from initial pickup to final delivery is one example. Tracking your luggage from the time you drop it off at the departure airport ticket counter until the time you pick it up at the baggage carousel at your final destination is another.

In general, this approach is well suited for monitoring any process in which there is a hand-off of responsibility from one participant to another. You give your luggage to the counter agent—one hand-off of responsibility. The counter agent places the bag on the conveyer as a means of handing off responsibility to the baggage handlers. The process continues until the final hand-off, which begins when the baggage handler at your final destination places the bag on the conveyer leading to the baggage carousel and ends when you pick up your luggage.

The events being monitored in track-and-trace situations are the evidence that individual hand-offs have been successful. The challenge in most situations is finding the evidence. In the days before security requirements mandated scanning and tracking luggage on airplanes, the evidence was scanty: You got your receipt for your bag when you dropped it off (that is, when you handed it off to the airline) and you (hopefully) picked up your bag at its destination. There was little evidence available for any intermediate progress.

The security requirement that luggage not travel on a plane unless the associated passenger is also on board has resulted in better tracking—better evidence—of your luggage's progress. The luggage tracking tag is scanned when the luggage is loaded on the plane or placed in a bin that will subsequently be loaded on the plane. It is scanned again when it comes off. These scans provide intermediate evidence of progress.

Your challenge in designing a Track-and-Trace solution is going to be finding appropriate evidence of progress. It is not uncommon that the full set of evidence you would like to have is simply not available. When this occurs, you may want to implement the degree of tracking that is supported by the currently available evidence and independently begin an initiative that will eventually provide more detailed evidence of progress. This is exactly what happened in the telecommunications case study described back in Chapter 2.

Business Process Timeliness Monitor

The Business Process Timeliness Monitor (Figure 3-9) is an extension of the Track-and-Trace pattern. State machine models can be extended so that the absence of an expected event within some period of time can be recognized. While, of course, you can apply this approach to recognizing that an overall process did not complete on time, the greatest benefit comes from recognizing that some intermediate event did not occur on time, and thus the overall process is in jeopardy of being late. The recognition can be used to trigger an action that will correct the course of the overall process and get it back on track for an on-time completion. The telecommunications case study discussed back in Chapter 2 is an example of this pattern in action.

Detecting the absence of an event requires the establishment of a service-level agreement specifying the maximum amount of time it should take for the process to complete or remain in each intermediate state. When the state machine monitoring the process is started or a particular intermediate state is entered, a timer is started. When the overall process completes, or the intermediate state is exited, the corresponding timer is stopped. However, if the timer expires before the

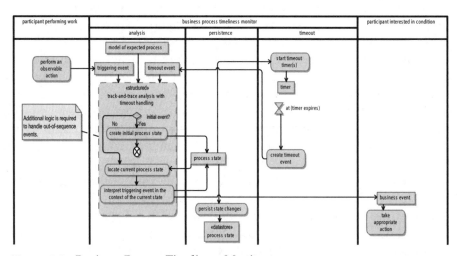

Figure 3-9: *Business Process Timeliness Monitor*

process completes or the intermediate state is exited, a timeout event is generated. This is an indication that some expected event did not occur.

In recognizing this situation, it is the expiration of the timer that serves as the trigger for the analysis. Some introspection of the state machine may be required to identify which events did not occur, but the larger design requirement is to determine which parties should be notified when this situation arises and what actions those parties are going to take to get the overall process back on track.

Situational Response

All the patterns in this chapter up to this point have had one characteristic in common: They simply recognize that some condition exists and announce that fact with an event. Other independent participants receive these notifications and decide what action to take.

In some situations there is an additional challenge in determining what the appropriate response ought to be (Figure 3-10). Further analysis is required, generally to focus the actions on achieving specific business objectives. Reference data, often containing historical information, is required for the analysis. The result of the analysis is generally one or more directives to actually perform the identified actions.

Consider the case in which there is some form of perishable commodity being sold: fresh produce and meat, seats on a plane, or hotel rooms—anything that becomes worthless if not sold by some point in

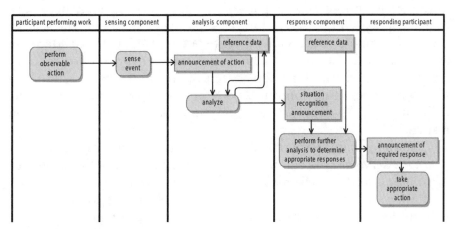

Figure 3-10: *Situational Response Pattern*

time. The desired business strategy is to dynamically set the price of the commodity based on the remaining inventory and the time remaining before the commodity becomes worthless. The situation being responded to in these cases is the presence of a potential consumer for the perishable commodity.

The simplistic approach to pricing the commodity is to fix a point in time at which it will be put on sale. The idea is that this will raise demand and ensure that the commodity does not go to waste. The problem with this approach is that it neither maximizes revenue nor minimizes the likelihood that the commodity will go to waste. If the commodity is selling well and will likely sell out, putting it on sale will result in lost revenue. On the other hand, if the commodity is selling very poorly, lowering the price by a set amount at a fixed point in time might not ensure that the commodity actually sells out.

A more sophisticated approach is to track the rate at which the commodity is selling versus the price of the commodity. With this approach, the offering price for the commodity can be adjusted dynamically. This approach is often applied to online product sales. It requires complex-event processing to do the dynamic price adjustments as consumers shop and as commodity inventories change. Note that the rate of sales and the current inventory become part of the reference data—a dynamic part whose currency must be maintained in a timely manner—most likely via events!

Decision as a Service

In the Decision-as-a-Service pattern (Figure 3-11), the logic necessary to make a decision is factored into a separate component. The service consumer gathers all relevant current-state input data for the decision and passes it to the service. This is typically a synchronous request-reply interaction, but it may be asynchronous. In either case, the decision service computes output data from the input data, using static reference data as appropriate. The output data reflects the decision results.

The value of this pattern is that it encapsulates the logic of the decision as a service. This simplifies the maintenance of both the service consumer and the decision service. In particular, it allows the implementation of the service (that is, the business rules) to be updated without requiring a modification to the service consumer.

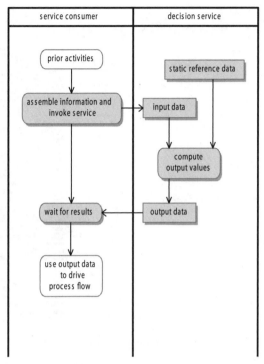

Figure 3-11: *Decision-as-a-Service Pattern*

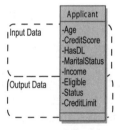

Figure 3-12: *Credit Card Decision Service Data Structure*

To make this possible, however, both the input and output data structures have to remain fixed.

Let's consider an example from the banking world. A bank needs to evaluate applications for credit cards to determine whether a credit card should be issued and what the credit limit should be on the account. In this case, the same data structure is used for both the input and output, with the difference being that some of the field values are computed by the Credit Card Decision service. Figure 3-12 shows this data structure. The input data includes the applicant's age, credit score,

ID	applicant.Age	applicant.CreditScore	applicant.HasDL	applicant.maritalStatus	applicant.Income	applicant.Eligible	applicant.Status	applicant.CreditLimit
1	0					false	invalidData	0.0
2	>= 16 && < 18	> 0 && < 500	true			true	rejected	0.0
3	>= 16 && < 18	>= 500 && < 600	true	single	> 0 && < 100000	true	rejected	0.0
4	>= 16 && < 18	>= 500 && < 600	true	married	> 0 && < 100000	true	pending	0.0
5	>= 16 && < 18	>= 500 && < 600	true		>=100000	true	accepted	500.0
6	>= 16 && < 18		false			false	notEligible	0.0
7	>= 16 && < 18	>= 600 && < 700	true		> 0 && < 100000	true	accepted	2000.0
8	>= 16 && < 18	>= 600 && < 700	true		>100000	true	accepted	3000.0
9	>= 16 && < 18	>= 700 && <= 850	true		> 0 && < 100000	true	accepted	4000.0
10	>= 16 && < 18	>= 700 && <= 850	true		>=100000	true	accepted	5000.0
11	>= 16 && < 18			divorced		true	rejected	0.0
12	>= 16 && < 18	0				false	invalidData	0.0
13	>= 16 && < 18				0	false	invalidData	0.0
14	>= 18 && < 26	> 0 && < 500				true	rejected	0.0
15	>= 18 && < 26	>= 500 && < 600		single	> 0 && < 100000	true	rejected	0.0
16	>= 18 && < 26	>= 500 && < 600		married	> 0 && < 100000	true	pending	0.0
17	>= 18 && < 26	>= 500 && < 600			>=100000	true	accepted	2000.0
18	>= 18 && < 26	>= 600 && < 700			> 0 && < 100000	true	accepted	5000.0
19	>= 18 && < 26	>= 600 && < 700			>=100000	true	accepted	7000.0
20	>= 18 && < 26	>= 700 && <= 850			> 0 && < 100000	true	accepted	8000.0
22	>= 18 && < 26	0				false	invalidData	0.0
23	>= 18 && < 26				0	false	invalidData	0.0
24	>= 26 && < 75	> 0 && < 500			> 0 && < 100000	true	rejected	0.0
25	>= 26 && < 75	> 0 && < 500		single	>=100000	true	rejected	0.0
26	>= 26 && < 75	> 0 && < 500		married	>=100000	true	pending	0.0
27	>= 26 && < 75	>= 500 && < 600		single	> 0 && < 100000	true	rejected	0.0
28	>= 26 && < 75	>= 500 && < 600		married	> 0 && < 100000	true	pending	0.0
29	>= 26 && < 75	>= 500 && < 600			>=100000	true	accepted	2000.0
30	>= 26 && < 75	>= 600 && < 700			> 0 && < 100000	true	accepted	5000.0
31	>= 26 && < 75	>= 600 && < 700			>=100000	true	accepted	7000.0
32	>= 26 && < 75	>= 700 && <= 850			> 0 && < 100000	true	accepted	11000.0
33	>= 26 && < 75	>= 700 && <= 850			>=100000	true	accepted	20000.0
34	>= 26 && < 75	0				false	invalidData	0.0
35	>= 26 && < 75				0	false	invalidData	0.0

Figure 3-13: *Decision Table for the Credit Card Decision Service*

a flag indicating whether or not the applicant has a driver's license, another flag indicating whether they are married, and the applicant's income. The computed output values comprise a Boolean indicating whether the applicant is eligible, a field indicating the current status, and another field indicating the credit limit should the status be accepted.

A decision table describing the logic for this service is shown in Figure 3-13. This example is developed using the TIBCO BusinessEvents® Decision Manager, which is described in Chapter 10. Each line of the table defines a set of conditions for the input values (the Condition Area) and the corresponding computed output values (the Action Area).

The Decision-as-a-Service pattern is useful when the business rules change frequently but the data used to drive the decision and the outputs of the decision can be fixed.

Orchestrated Response

While process orchestration is not a traditional focus of complex-event processing, the need to orchestrate portions of CEP solution activity is increasing in importance (Figure 3-14). In this relatively common

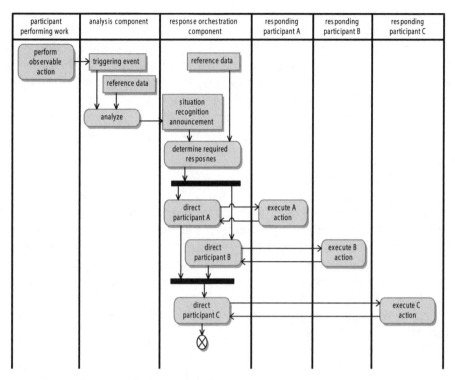

Figure 3-14: *Response Orchestration Pattern*

pattern, process orchestration is used to coordinate multiple participants in responding to a situation. The reason for the orchestration is twofold: to control the order in which the actions are performed and to confirm the successful completion of the actions. Less common is a situation in which process coordination is required for situation recognition.

This pattern is a hybrid of event-driven and request-driven interactions. All of the interactions up to the receipt of the situation recognition announcement are event driven. The response orchestration component, however, uses request-driven interactions to not only request that each participant perform its work but also to confirm the successful completion of that work.

When this pattern is used, a choice must be made regarding the type of technology to be used for the response orchestration. Traditionally, this would be a component designed specifically for process orchestration, such as TIBCO ActiveMatrix BusinessWorks™ or TIBCO ActiveMatrix® BPM. With this approach, if rule-based reasoning is required in the orchestration, the Decision-as-a-Service pattern is used. The service returns values that then guide the subsequent process execution.

However, separating process orchestration from complex-event processing may become a performance barrier, particularly if a significant amount of repetitive information must be passed to the decision service on each invocation. In such cases, it is better to have the process orchestration performed directly by a CEP component. This is the purpose of the TIBCO BusinessEvents® Process Orchestration product. It adds process orchestration capabilities to TIBCO BusinessEvents®.

Pioneering Solutions

We close this chapter on a cautionary note. Early explorers drew maps of the territories they became familiar with and drew dragons in the unexplored corners of these maps, warning those later map readers to beware of those unexplored spaces. Even worse, many explorers never even reached their goals: Columbus was seeking Asia when he found the Americas, and numerous explorers sought unsuccessfully for the Northwest Passage that would provide a North American route from the Atlantic to the Pacific.

The relevance here is that there are many types of applications for complex-event processing that have been well explored. If you are working in one of these areas, the problem is well defined, and implementing your solution will be a straightforward engineering exercise. If, however, you are working in an area that is not well defined, one in which the analytical approach for either situation recognition or action determination has not yet been established, proceed with caution. Some (but not all) of these areas are true research topics—you need to invest a little time in determining whether or not your particular problem is well defined before you commit to building a solution. Remember, it took more than 400 years to find the Northwest Passage!

How can you tell when you are on safe ground? Ask yourself the following questions:

- Is the information related to the problem understood well enough to create a quality information model (including relevant state information)?
- Is there a well-defined (i.e., measurable) set of criteria that defines the situation that needs to be recognized?
- Are there well-defined triggers that identify the points in time at which the situation recognition analysis will be performed?

- Is the information necessary for this recognition analysis readily accessible?
- Is there a clearly articulated approach for using the available information to recognize the situation?
- Is there a well-defined (i.e., measurable) approach for responding to the situation once it has been recognized?
- Is the reference information needed for determining the response readily accessible?
- Does the business value of the resulting situation recognition and response capabilities warrant the investment in the solution?

If you answered yes to all of these questions, you are on solid ground. If you answered no to any of them, you may be plowing new ground. You need to eliminate this uncertainty before you commit to producing a solution. Focus your initial efforts on developing the answers to these questions, with particular attention to the last one: Is the result worth the effort? Then, and only then, should you commit to building a solution.

The riskiest question in the list is the first: What is it that you are trying to recognize? Define your goals based on solid analytical results and beware of open-ended criteria. For example, you are never going to recognize all forms of financial fraud: The bad guys are constantly inventing new ways to scam the financial system and circumvent the checks currently in place. Identifying fraud, in general, is not an achievable goal.

On the other hand, there are specific behavior patterns that fairly reliably indicate that there might be fraud in progress. An analysis of login patterns might identify these behavior patterns, and the recognition of these patterns as they occur is definitely a well-defined and measurable goal.

If you find yourself waving your hands as you attempt to get specific about defining your recognition goals—stop! You are treading on thin ice. Do your analytical homework and convince yourself that you can be precise about what is to be recognized.

Summary

There are two factors that contribute to the variability in complex-event processing architectures. One is the handling of reference data and the extent to which the stream of events modifies the reference data used to interpret subsequent events. The other is the myriad ways in which the necessary sense, analyze, and respond activities can be partitioned and assigned to components. There is no one-size-fits-all architecture for complex event processing.

The simplest architectures are those in which the reference data is not impacted by the stream of events. The Threshold Detection and Condition Detection patterns are examples of these.

When the event stream can alter the reference data, the architecture gets a bit more complicated. The reference data now contains some historical information. If this information is essential for analysis, the solution must now become a system of record for this information. This requires persisting the information.

The Situation Recognition pattern uses historical data in its analysis. Some of the events that arrive simply result in updates to the historical data. Others, when analyzed, signify the recognition of a business-significant condition that must be announced. Track-and-Trace is a specialization of this pattern that does milestone-level tracking of a process. The Business Process Timeliness Monitor extends Track-and-Trace to determine whether the milestones are achieved on time.

Some applications require more than simply announcing that a condition exists. The Situational Response pattern applies contextual analysis to determine the actions that are required in a specific situation. The Decision-as-a-Service pattern makes these analytical capabilities available to non-CEP components. Sometimes the requirement extends beyond simply identifying the required actions to include the management of their execution. The result is the Orchestrated Response pattern.

Building a solution in which the situations to be recognized, the desired responses, and the analytical techniques to be used are all well defined is a straightforward (though sometimes complex) engineering exercise. Building a solution when any of these is not well defined has a significant degree of uncertainty. In these situations, before a commitment is made to produce a solution, preliminary work should be undertaken to clarify the approach to recognition and response. Once this preliminary work has been completed, an estimate of the effort required to implement the solution should be made to ensure that it is warranted by the expected business benefit.

Part II

Technology

Chapter 4

TIBCO BusinessEvents®

Objectives

TIBCO BusinessEvents® is a product suite that supports complex event processing. This chapter provides an overview of the product suite, describing the base product and its five available functional extensions. It also describes the life cycle of a TIBCO BusinessEvents project. The five chapters following this one are devoted to a more detailed examination of the internal product architecture.

TIBCO BusinessEvents® Product Suite

The TIBCO BusinessEvents® product suite consists of six products (Figure 4-1). The core product is TIBCO BusinessEvents itself. The five functional extensions are TIBCO BusinessEvents® Views, TIBCO BusinessEvents® Data Modeling, TIBCO BusinessEvents® Decision Manager, TIBCO BusinessEvents® Event Stream Processing, and TIBCO BusinessEvents® Process Orchestration. The core product, TIBCO BusinessEvents, is required for all of the functional extensions.

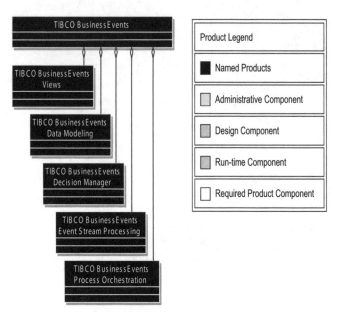

Figure 4-1: *TIBCO BusinessEvents Product Suite*

TIBCO BusinessEvents®

The core product, TIBCO BusinessEvents® (Figure 4-2) provides basic event processing, a rules engine, and the modeling of concepts and events. The primary run-time component is the *processing unit*, which is a Java virtual machine (JVM) configured to support functional units known as *agents*. The core product provides two types of agents. *Inference agents* provide the functionality for processing rules. *Cache agents* provide a distributed data grid that can extend across multiple processing units. There are three additional kinds of agents that are part of the functional extensions described later.

TIBCO BusinessEvents comes with TIBCO BusinessEvents® Studio, an eclipse-based design environment with an integrated debugger. It provides two administrative options. One is the TIBCO Administrator™ and its supporting TIBCO Runtime Agent™. The other is the TIBCO BusinessEvents Monitoring and Management component (BEMM).

An optional component is the rules management server. This server, along with its associated web studio interface, provides the ability to change values used in rules at runtime.

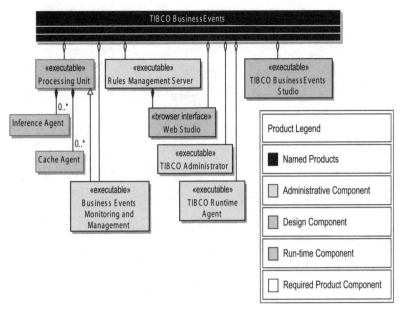

Figure 4-2: *TIBCO BusinessEvents®*

TIBCO BusinessEvents® Data Modeling

TIBCO BusinessEvents® Data Modeling is an extension to TIBCO BusinessEvents that adds capabilities in two areas: data modeling and state machine modeling (Figure 4-3).

The data modeling capabilities include the ability for the TIBCO BusinessEvents Studio to import relational database schema definitions and automatically define the corresponding memory-resident TIBCO BusinessEvents concepts (these are discussed in Chapter 5). Functional extensions are added to the inference agent, which enable it to query and update the database. Functional extensions are added to the cache agent, which enable it to load information from the database into the cache. Transactional interactions with the database are supported.

The state modeling capabilities include the ability to define a state machine using UML 1.2 state machine notation. State machine representations are used to model business processes and the life cycles of concepts (these are discussed further in Chapter 5). State machine modeling capabilities include the modeling of timeouts (the failure to reach

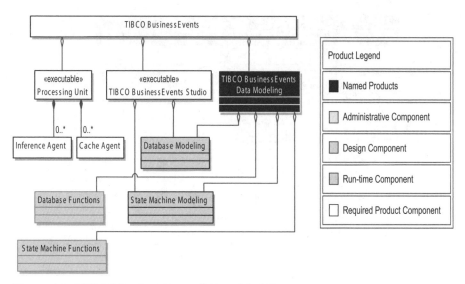

Figure 4-3: *TIBCO BusinessEvents® Data Modeling*

a given state within a period of time). This makes it possible to identify events that should have happened, but did not, and take appropriate action.

Figure 4-4 shows a state machine model for the handling of luggage by an airline. This model can then be used to keep track of the state of each individual piece of luggage as it moves through the system.

TIBCO BusinessEvents® Decision Manager

TIBCO BusinessEvents® Decision Manager (Figure 4-5) is an extension to TIBCO BusinessEvents that is designed to make it possible for business users to define business rules. It includes a plugin for the TIBCO BusinessEvents Studio that provides a spreadsheet-style interface for defining and testing business rules. It provides facilities to import and export rules from Microsoft® Excel spreadsheets so that business users can work with spreadsheets directly. The studio extension can check rules for both completeness and consistency, and can automatically generate test data from rules.

Also included is the Decision Manager Browser Interface is an extension to the Web Studio that enables the run-time updating of decision tables while the BusinessEvents solution is running.

Figure 4-6 shows the TIBCO BusinessEvents Studio user interface provided by the Decision Manager plugin. This interface is described in Chapter 5.

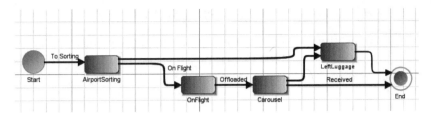

Figure 4-4: *State Model of Airline Luggage Handling*

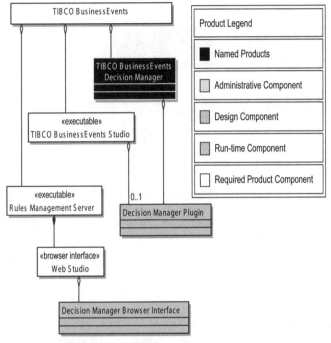

Figure 4-5: *TIBCO BusinessEvents® Decision Manager*

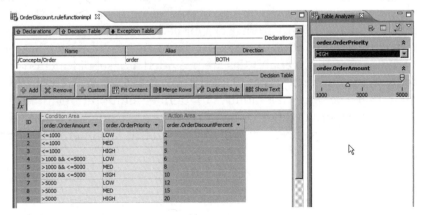

Figure 4-6: *TIBCO BusinessEvents Decision Manager User Interface*

TIBCO BusinessEvents® Event Stream Processing

TIBCO BusinessEvents® Event Stream Processing (Figure 4-7) is another functional extension to TIBCO BusinessEvents. It adds capabilities in two areas: queries and pattern matching.

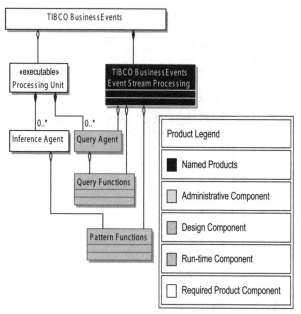

Figure 4-7: *TIBCO BusinessEvents® Event Stream Processing*

The query capabilities are packaged in a new kind of agent: the query agent. This agent provides both snapshot (on-demand) queries and continuous queries that are automatically reevaluated when their under-lying data changes. Queries are expressed using a subset of the Object Query Language (OQL) from the Object Data Management Group.[1] Queries and the operation of the query agent are described in Chapter 7.

Pattern matching capabilities are provided as a set of functions that execute in the inference agent. Patterns are described in an English-like format that includes the ability to define temporal relationships. Actions can be initiated both when the pattern is recognized and when an event occurs that does not match the pattern. The operation of pat-terns is described in Chapter 11.

---

1. http://www.odbms.org/odmg/

TIBCO BusinessEvents® Process Orchestration

TIBCO BusinessEvents® Process Orchestration adds to TIBCO BusinessEvents the ability to orchestrate activities (Figure 4-8). The orchestration is performed by a new type of agent, the *process agent*. The process is defined using a Business Process Modeling Notation (BPMN) plugin for the TIBCO BusinessEvents Studio. The definitions of processes and the operation of the process agent are described in Chapter 8.

TIBCO BusinessEvents® Views

TIBCO BusinessEvents® Views (Figure 4-9) is a functional extension to the core TIBCO BusinessEvents product. It enables the real-time display of information in both graphical and tabular form. These displays make it convenient to visualize levels of activity or processing trends as well as to provide a mechanism for using visual alerts to bring attention to exceptions.

The extension provides a new kind of agent, the dashboard agent, along with a browser-based interface (Figure 4-10) for the information display. It also provides an extended version of the processing unit—a separate `be-views.exe` executable. This executable must be used whenever the dashboard agent is used. The configuration and operation of the dashboard agent is described in Chapter 9.

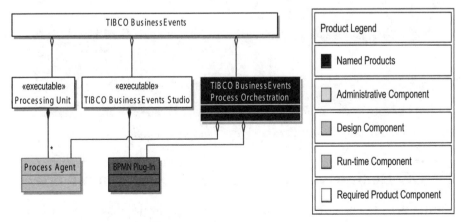

Figure 4-8: *TIBCO BusinessEvents® Process Orchestration*

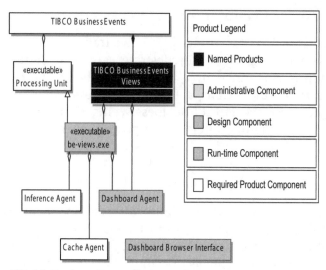

Figure 4-9: *TIBCO BusinessEvents® Views*

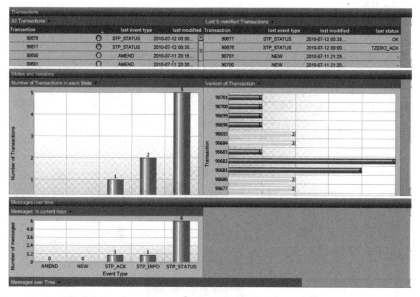

Figure 4-10: *TIBCO BusinessEvents® Views Display Example*

TIBCO BusinessEvents® Solution Deployment

Solutions based on TIBCO BusinessEvents are deployed in one or more processing units, which are Java virtual machines (JVMs) configured to host the various types of agents (Figure 4-11). Processing units are logically grouped together in what is known as a *cluster*. The processing units in the cluster all share a common multicast or unicast group that provides the mechanism by which the engines communicate with one another.

Each processing unit contains one or more agents. Between the base product and its five extensions, there are five available types of agents: inference agents, cache agents, query agents, process agents, and dashboard agents. The inference agent provides the basic event and rule processing structure. The cache agent manages a cache of information and coordinates the sharing of this information across multiple processing units. The query agent manages the queries being executed against the cache. The process agent orchestrates the execution of activities, both internal and external. The dashboard agent manages the graphical and tabular display of information. The operation of each agent is described in Chapters 5 through 9.

While each processing unit is capable of hosting multiple types of agents, there are some restrictions imposed by the product itself and some further best practice constraints that limit the combinations of agent types that are deployed in a given processing unit.

The chief restriction is that inference agents and cache agents cannot be deployed in the same processing unit.[2] There is also a best practice recommendation to run query agents in their own processing units. Following these restrictions leads to the typical application deployment shown in Figure 4-12. Note that there may be multiple instances of each type of processing unit.

As of this writing, process agents cannot be deployed in the same cluster as inference agents. Since most of the functional capabilities of the inference agent are available within the process agent, this is not as significant a restriction as it seems on the surface. Chapter 8 provides more details.

It is a best practice recommendation that dashboard agents and the inference and cache agents involved in managing the displayed information be deployed in a separate cluster. The reason for this is that maintaining the real-time information display can be resource intensive. Placing the display-related components in a separate cluster from the application enables the resources for each to be managed separately.

---

2. There is an override for this restriction that is intended for use only in development.

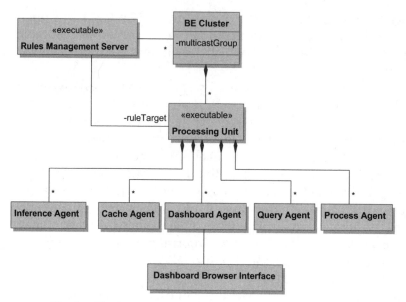

Figure 4-11: *Deployable Components*

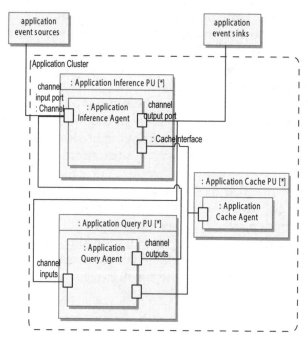

Figure 4-12: *Typical Application Deployment*

BusinessEvents Solution Life Cycle

A TIBCO BusinessEvents solution begins its life in the TIBCO BusinessEvents Studio (Figure 4-13). Here the solution design is created and saved in an EAR file, and the deployment description is captured in a CDD file. These files are then picked up by the TIBCO Administrator. During deployment, the administrator communicates using TIBCO Rendezvous® or TIBCO Enterprise Message Service™ (EMS) with the TIBCO Runtime Agent (TRA) on each machine on which a processing unit will be deployed. The TRA places the required configuration information on the local machine's file system, executes command lines to start and stop engines, and communicates with the engines to obtain status information.

Figure 4-14 details the interactions between these components during the life cycle. The TIBCO BusinessEvents Studio is used to design the application, with the design being saved in an EAR file. It is also used to define the packaging of the application components for deployment, with this packaging being saved in a cluster deployment descriptor (CDD) file. From the TIBCO Administrator these files are uploaded. Once the EAR file has been loaded, its properties and global variables can be set in

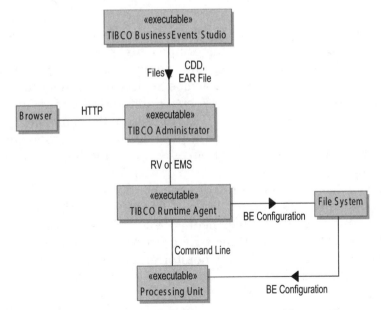

Figure 4-13: *TIBCO BusinessEvents® Administrative Architecture Pattern*

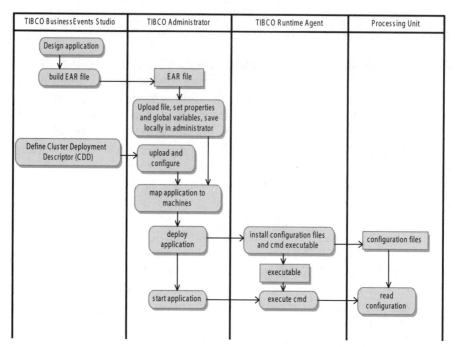

Figure 4-14: *Solution Deployment Process*

preparation for deployment. Similarly, once the CDD file has been uploaded, the deployment of the components on individual machines can be specified. Upon deployment, the administrator communicates with the TRA on each involved machine to place both configuration files and executables on the machine. When the administrator starts the application, it instructs each involved TRA to execute the command line for each processing unit to be started. Upon start-up, each processing unit reads its configuration files from the local machine and begins processing.

TIBCO BusinessEvents provides another deployment and management option: TIBCO BusinessEvents® Monitoring and Management (MM). Monitoring and Management is, itself, a TIBCO BusinessEvents-based application, comprising two processing units and a TIBCO Hawk® agent (Figure 4-15). To monitor an application, MM requires the same EAR and CDD files that would have been used by the TIBCO Administrator to manage the application. MM can then directly manage the application's processing units in a cluster. It uses SSH to deploy the processing units. It uses SSH or Hawk to start and stop processing

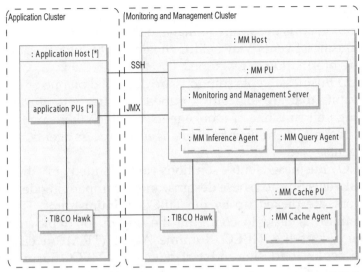

Figure 4-15: *TIBCO BusinessEvents® Monitoring and Management (MM) Deployment*

units, and JMX to start, stop, and pause individual agents and enable and disable rules within an agent. It uses Hawk to collect performance data and monitor the health of the application cluster.

Both the TIBCO Administrator and TIBCO BusinessEvents Monitoring and Manager provide the ability for scripted deployments. Please consult the product manuals for more details on these options.

Summary

The TIBCO BusinessEvents product suite consists of the TIBCO BusinessEvents product and five extension products: TIBCO BusinessEvents Data Modeling, TIBCO BusinessEvents Decision Manager, TIBCO BusinessEvents Event Stream Processing, TIBCO BusinessEvents Process Orchestration, and TIBCO BusinessEvents Views. TIBCO BusinessEvents Data Modeling enables caching database information in memory for use by TIBCO BusinessEvents and adds state machine modeling capability. TIBCO Business Events Decision Manager adds spreadsheet-style interfaces for defining rules and the ability to change those rules at runtime. TIBCO BusinessEvents Event Stream Processing adds query capabilities and the ability to

recognize patterns of events. TIBCO Business Events Process
Orchestration adds the ability to manage the performance of activities.
TIBCO BusinessEvents Views adds the ability to display tabular and
graphical information in real time.

TIBCO BusinessEvents solutions are deployed on one or more processing units that are logically grouped together into clusters. Each
processing unit runs one or more agents, of which there are five types:
inference agents, cache agents, query agents, process agents, and dashboard agents.

TIBCO BusinessEvents solutions are defined in the TIBCO
BusinessEvents Studio. These designs, and accompanying deployment
descriptors, are picked up by the TIBCO Administrator. The TIBCO
Administrator is used to configure the design for deployment and,
with the aid of the TIBCO Runtime Agent (TRA) on each target
machine, deploy the design and start the engines. TIBCO BusinessEvents
Monitoring and Management (BEMM) and scripts provide alternative
approaches for deployment and monitoring.

Chapter 5

Inference Agents

Objectives

The inference agent is the heart of TIBCO BusinessEvents®. It provides analytical capabilities for complex event processing, staging information in memory and operating on that information with rules. It interacts with its external environment through a variety of channels through which it can both sense and respond to activity in its environment.

After reading this chapter you will be able to describe

- The role of the inference agent in TIBCO BusinessEvents

- How information is represented in the form of event, concept, and scorecard data structures

- How events, concepts, and scorecards are created and consumed in an inference agent

- How rules are structured and operate on events, concepts, and scorecards

- How an inference agent uses channels to interact with its external environment

- The threading model of the inference agent and the available tuning options

Inference Agent Overview

There's quite a bit to the inference agent, and to present it all at once would be confusing. We'll start with the simplified overview of Figure 5-1 and then add components until the picture is complete.

The functional heart of the inference agent is the run-to-completion function (RTC) that executes the rules. It operates on events, concepts, and scorecards being held in working memory. Channels provide both input and output capabilities, and the cache interface provides for information sharing between agents. We'll get to the channels and the cache later on, but for now let's look at how information is represented in the working memory and analyzed by the RTC function executing rules.

Events, Concepts, and Scorecards

There are three primary memory-resident data structures used by the inference agent: events, concepts, and scorecards (Figure 5-2). Events are static representations of information characterizing an event, whether it is an event originating elsewhere or one that originates within the inference agent. Events, once placed in working memory, are not editable.

Concepts are representations of information, other than events, that is required by the rules. This may be information imported from other sources or accumulated and maintained by inference agents

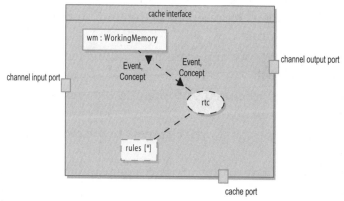

Figure 5-1: *Inference Agent Simplified View*

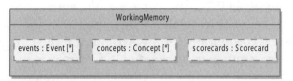

Figure 5-2: *Working Memory*

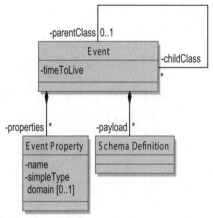

Figure 5-3: *Event Data Structure*

and other parties. In contrast with events, concepts are editable: Rules can modify concepts.

Scorecards are a special kind of concept generally used for accumulating summary information.

The following sections explore these data structures and their intended usage.

Events

An event data structure (Figure 5-3) is intended to be a representation of an event: a snapshot of a situation at some point in time. Be sure to name your events so that they are descriptive of the situation whose occurrence they are intended to represent. Events can have a `timeTo-Live`, some `properties`, and a `payload`. Events can also be subclassed from other events.

The `timeToLive` parameter indicates, as the name implies, how long the event data structure will persist. A positive value, expressed in a time unit, indicates the period of time during which the event data structure will remain available. A value of zero indicates that the event data structure will remain around only until the first RTC cycle completes. A negative value indicates that the event data structure will remain until it is explicitly deleted. The implications of selecting values for the `timeToLive` parameter are explored in the Chapter 6 discussion of memory management modes. Of course, any event may be explicitly removed at any time by calling the `consumeEvent()` catalog function.

Event `properties` are named values that have a simple data type: `String`, `int`, `long`, `double`, `boolean`, or `DateTime`. Optionally, the values can be restricted so that they can only be taken from an enumeration of values provided by the indicated domain. Event properties are efficiently accessed by conditional expressions in rules.

The event `payload` is an optional data structure whose structure is specified by an XML schema definition (XSD). Elements of the payload can be referenced in rules using xPath expressions, but this access is not as efficient as accessing properties. For this reason, when elements of the payload need to be accessed in rules and performance is a significant consideration, it is common practice to copy those element values into properties at the time the event is created. This is done during preprocessing, which is discussed later in this chapter.

With two exceptions, an event is local to the agent that created it (other types of agents can create events as well). One of these exceptions is an event that is explicitly sent externally via a channel. The other is an event with a non-zero `timeToLive` that was also declared to use the `Cache-Only` memory management mode (described in Chapter 6). Such an event will be visible to a query running in a query agent (Chapter 7). With these two exceptions, an event is strictly local to the agent that creates it.

Figure 5-4 shows three related events. The parent `Transaction` event has properties that indicate the `amount` of the transaction and

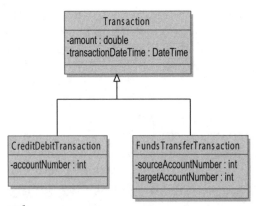

Figure 5-4: *Event Example*

the `transactionDateTime`. There are two sub-classes as well. The `CreditDebitTransaction` sub-class adds an `accountNumber` property to indicate the account from which the funds were taken or added. The `FundsTransferTransaction` has two account number properties: the `sourceAccountNumber` to indicate the account from which the funds were taken and the `targetAccountNumber` to indicate the account to which the funds were added.

Concepts

A concept is an editable data structure that can be used for many purposes (Figure 5-5). The name of the concept should indicate what the concept is intended to represent. Each concept instance has an optional external identifier (`extID`) property that can be set at the time the concept is instantiated.[1] It is good practice to assign a value to the `extID` that is unique across all concept instances. It serves as a unique identifier that can be used for retrieving the concept when needed (discussed later in this chapter) and also serves as a key for locking the concept when locking is required (discussed in Chapter 6).

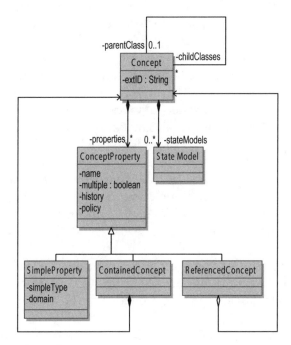

Figure 5-5: *Concept Data Structure*

1. All objects in TIBCO BusinessEvents® actually have this property, but it is particularly important on concepts.

Concepts have a set of properties. Each property has a `name`, which must be unique within the concept. Properties may have multiple values associated with them, as indicated by the `multiple` flag. A person, for example, might have several alternative names (i.e., aliases).

A property can also maintain a `history` of previous values. An `Account` concept, for example, might have a `balance` property, and it might be useful to have a history of previous account balances for statistical or analytical purposes. History is specified by giving the number of historical values to be kept. The `policy` property determines whether all historical values are kept (even when the value does not change) or only different values are kept. There are some limitations on the use of history. One is that rule conditions can only access history via catalog functions, and the use of these functions in conditions is inefficient. Another is that when XML representations of concepts are automatically generated, history is not included.

Properties can be of three types: simple types, contained concepts, and referenced concepts. Simple types are the same as for events: `String`, `int`, `long`, `double`, `boolean`, or `DateTime`. Optionally, these values can be constrained to be values found in a specified `domain`.

Contained concepts are owned by their parent concept, and a contained concept can only be owned by one parent concept. Instances of contained concepts share the same lifetime as their parent instances. Deleting the parent instance also deletes the contained instance. However, contained instances can be added and removed without affecting the lifetime of the parent instance.

Referenced concepts are pointers to concepts. A concept may be referenced by many other concepts. There is no connection between the lifetime of the referenced instance and that of the holder of the reference—either may be deleted without impacting the other. However, if the referenced instance is deleted, the reference becomes a null pointer.

Figure 5-6 shows three example concepts, all related to a bank account. The `Account` has an `accountNumber` property and a `balance` property. In this context, a history of the account balance might be of interest.

The `Account` contains `Transaction` concepts that record the `amount` and the `dateTime` of each transaction. The `Transaction` concept provides a persistent record of the transaction, in contrast to the `Transaction` event from Figure 5-4 that simply announced the

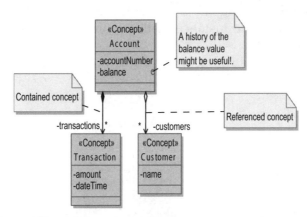

Figure 5-6: *Concept Example*

occurrence of a transaction elsewhere. Typically, it would be the arrival of the `Transaction` event that would result in the creation of the `Transaction` concept and its addition to the list of `Account trans-actions`. The use of the contained concept relationship here means that should an `Account` instance be deleted, all of the contained `Transaction` concept instances would also be deleted.

The `Account` also has references to the `Customer` concept. The use of the reference allows a `Customer` instance to be added or removed from an `Account` instance, and this further allows an `Account` instance to be deleted without requiring the deletion of the `Customer` instance.

Scorecards

A scorecard is a special kind of concept (Figure 5-7). It only has properties of a simple data type, defined in the same manner as the simple properties of a concept. What is unique about a scorecard is that there is exactly one instance of a scorecard in each inference agent instance. The scorecard is generally used to summarize activity within that infer-ence agent instance.

For example, if an inference agent were detecting potential fraud on bank accounts, you might want to keep track of the number of fraud reports that each inference agent had generated (Figure 5-8). A FraudScorecard with a numberOfFraudReports property could be used to keep track of this. You might then have the agent periodically pub-lish an event containing the count to date and reset the count to zero. Some other component would then receive those publications and sum the numbers to obtain an overall count of the number of fraud reports.

If three inference agents were deployed with this fraud scorecard, you would have one instance of this scorecard in each of the three agents (Figure 5-9).

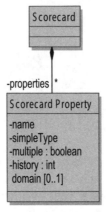

Figure 5-7: *Scorecard Data Structure*

Figure 5-8: *Fraud Scorecard Example*

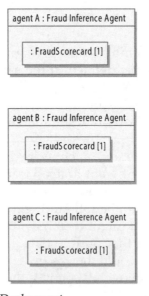

Figure 5-9: *Fraud Scorecard Deployment*

Rules

A rule in TIBCO BusinessEvents (Listing 5-1) has four clauses: attributes, declarations, conditions, and actions.

Listing 5-1: *Fraud Rule with Conditions Separate*

```
rule Rules.Fraud {
  attribute {priority = 5; forwardChain = true; }
  declare {
    Events.Transaction transA;
    Events.Transaction transB;
  }
  when {
    transB.transactionAmount <= 5.0; /* C1 */
    transA.transactionAmount >= 10000; /* C2 */
    transA.accountNumber == transB.accountNumber; /* C3 */
    transA.transactionDateTime > transB.transactionDateTime ; /*
      C4 */
  }
  then {
    System.debugOut("Fraud!");
  }
}
```

Attributes

The attributes clause is marked by the `attribute` keyword. There are three possible attributes: `forwardChain`, `priority`, and `rank`. The `forwardChain` attribute determines whether object changes made by the rule will cause the rule agenda to be reevaluated. In general this attribute should always be set to `true`. The `priority` and `rank` attributes determine the relative order in which rules will be applied. The `priority` attribute is an integer whose value is fixed at design time. The `rank` attribute designates a rule function that will be called at runtime. This function returns a `double` value. Rules that are eligible to run are sorted with `priority` as the primary sort key and `rank` as a secondary sort key. This sorting occurs as part of the run-to-completion (RTC) cycle described later in this chapter.

Declarations

The declarations clause is marked by the `declare` keyword. It identifies, by type, the objects in the working memory that are used by the rule. These objects may be events, concepts, or scorecards. In this listing, the two declared objects are both `Transaction` events.

The declarations clause serves a second purpose as well: It identifies the objects whose changes (creations or modifications) will trigger the execution of the rule.

Conditions

The conditional clause is marked by the when keyword. It specifies the conditions that must be true before the actions clause will be executed. There are three basic types of conditions: filters, equivalent joins, and nonequivalent joins.

Filter conditions are comparisons between a value retrieved from an object and a constant value. In the example, the transaction-Amount property of the Transaction event is being compared with the constants 5.0 and 10000. From a computational perspective, filter conditions are the least expensive type of conditions.

Equivalent join conditions compare values or expressions from two objects to see if they are equivalent. In the example, the accountNumbers of two transactions are being compared to see if they are the same. Equivalent joins are more expensive than filter conditions, but less expensive than nonequivalent joins.

Nonequivalent join conditions compare values from two objects with an operator other than identity. In the example, the transactionDateTime values of the two transactions are compared to see whether one occurred after the other.

For efficiency, TIBCO BusinessEvents sorts the conditions, executing filter conditions first, then equivalent joins, and lastly, nonequivalent joins.

Multiple conditions can be combined together using "&&" and "||" Boolean operators, but this should be done with an understanding of how the inference agent will execute the rule conditions. This is discussed in more detail later in this chapter. The *TIBCO BusinessEvents®️ Developer's Guide* provides additional information.

Actions

The action clause is marked by the then keyword. It specifies the actions to be taken when the conditions are all true. There are many possible actions that can be taken, including

- Creating, modifying, and deleting concepts
- Modifying scorecards
- Creating and consuming events

- Calling external services
- Calling rule functions, virtual rule functions, catalog functions, and custom functions

Run-to-Completion (RTC) Behavior

The basic behavior of the run-to-completion function is shown in Figure 5-10. Some entity asserts events and concepts into the working memory (how this occurs will be discussed later). Objects that appear in equivalent join conditions are indexed on the values used for the

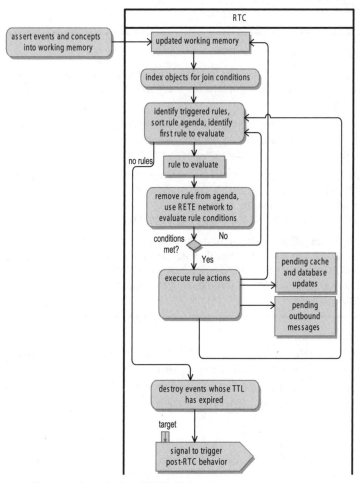

Figure 5-10: *Run-to-Completion (RTC) Behavior*

join as they are added to working memory. This greatly increases the efficiency of the equivalent join operation when it is eventually performed. Next, all of the rules that are triggered because of changes to events, concepts, or scorecards in the rule's declarations clause are identified. The triggered rules are then sorted by their priority and rank values, as described earlier. This sorted list is referred to as the *rule agenda*.

Once the rule agenda has been sorted, one rule is selected for evaluation and is removed from the rule agenda. The rule itself is used to construct what is known as a modified Rete network (see Rete Networks sidebar), which provides an efficient approach for evaluating rules against a set of objects. For each valid combination of input objects, the actions clause of the rule is then executed.

Rete Networks

A description of the original Rete concept can be found in Charles L. Forgy's classic paper, "Rete: A Fast Algorithm for the Many Pattern/Many Object Pattern Match Problem."[2]

However, the approach described in Forgy's paper does not cover rules whose conditions include joins between objects, including the equivalent and nonequivalent joins found in TIBCO BusinessEvents rules.

Networks that can process joins are referred to as modified Rete networks. Unfortunately, no publicly available papers describe the operations of such a network. Furthermore, a thorough discussion of such networks and the rationale behind them is well beyond the scope of this book.

The good news is that a detailed understanding of modified RETE networks is not really necessary to effectively use TIBCO BusinessEvents inference agents. You just need a general understanding of how conditional clauses are processed. This is provided in the form of examples in the discussion of the inference agent RTC behavior.

In the actions clause, any actions that require communications outside the scope of the inference agent are queued for later execution. Other actions may affect working memory: deleting events, modifying scorecards, and creating, updating, or deleting concepts.

2. Charles L. Forgy, "Rete: A Fast Algorithm for the Many Pattern/Many Object Pattern Match Problem," in *Artificial Intelligence*, vol. 19, pp. 17–37, North-Holland (1982).

Once all of the actions have been completed, the rule agenda is again evaluated and sorted. If `forwardChain = true`, changes to the working memory may cause rules to be added to or removed from the agenda. Since values of concept properties can be updated, and these values can be used in the computation of the rule's rank, even the sorting of the rule agenda may be altered.

This process continues until there are no more rules in the rule agenda. At this point any events whose time-to-live has expired (including all whose time-to-live is zero) are removed from the working memory. A signal is sent to the post-RTC threads to begin performing all of the pending communications resulting from executing the rule actions.

ACEPSTConditionsSeparate[3] Example

Let's take a look at an example using the `ACEPSTConditionsSeparate` project. This project implements the fraud rule from Listing 5-1. The run-time configuration of this project executing in the TIBCO BusinessEvents® Studio debugger is shown in Figure 5-11. This configuration has a single processing unit containing a single inference agent in which the fraud rule has been deployed. The debugger is then used to insert test data directly into the agent's working memory.

The test data for this project is shown in Figure 5-12.

The debugger inserts the test data transactions into the working memory where they are processed one at a time. The assertion of these transactions causes the fraud rule (Listing 5-1) to be placed in the rule agenda. When the rule is selected for processing, a RETE network is constructed to execute the conditional portions of the rule (Figure 5-13).

The first node in the Rete network is a filter node that is derived from the declarations clause of the rule. Each type mentioned in the clause results in a corresponding type filter in the Rete network. The type filter results are then fed to filters C1 and C2, each looking at the `amount` but each comparing it to a different value. The C1 and C2 result sets are the inputs to the C3 equivalent join node, where the two inputs are compared to see whether they have the same `account` value. The C3 results are fed to C4, a nonequivalent join node that compares the times of the two transactions. Anything that appears in the C4 result set has met all of the conditions and will have the rule actions applied to it.

---

3. All of the examples specific to this book are prefixed with the acronym ACEPST (Architecting Complex-Event Processing Solutions with TIBCO).

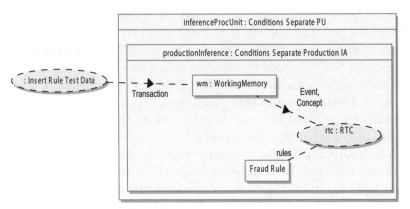

Figure 5-11: *ACEPSTConditionsSeparate Configuration*

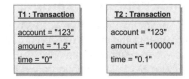

Figure 5-12: *ACEPSTConditionsSeparate Test Data*

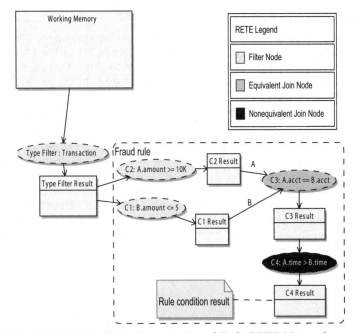

Figure 5-13: *ACEPSTConditionsSeparate Fraud Rule RETE Network*

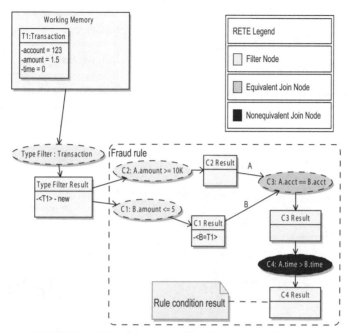

Figure 5-14: *ACEPSTConditionsSeparate First Transaction Processing*

Figure 5-14 shows the state of the Rete network after transaction T1 has been inserted into the working memory. Since T1 is of type Transaction, T1 ends up in the type filter result set. Since T1 has an amount less than 5, it ends up in the C1 result set, but not the C2 result set. Since C2 does not contain any results, there is no join for C3 to perform and processing stops.

Figure 5-15 shows the state after the T2 is introduced. Note that the results from processing T1 still present. T2 passes through the type filter and ends up in the type filter result set. Since Rete processing is driven entirely by changes, only the newly present T2 will be processed by the C1 and C2 filters, and T2 ends up in the C2 result set. Now the C3 equivalent join has two transactions to compare. Since they have the same account value, the pair T1 and T2 end up in the C3 result set. The appearance of the pair now triggers the evaluation of the C4 non-equivalent join. Since the time conditions are met, the pair end up in the C4 result set. The presence of results in the C4 result set now triggers the execution of the actions associated with the fraud rule.

Rule Conditions and Rete Network Efficiency

The rule shown in Listing 5-1 has each of the conditions as a separate clause ending with a semicolon. This separation of clauses allows a

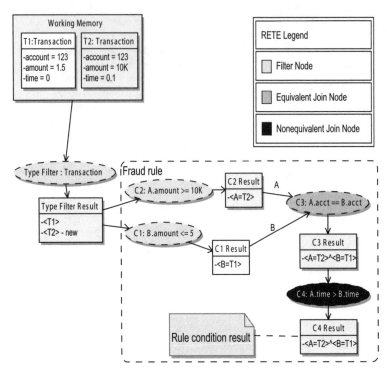

Figure 5-15: *ACEPSTConditionsSeparate Second Transaction Processing*

Rete network to be constructed with the relatively efficient filter nodes first, followed by the equivalent join nodes and ending up with the inefficient nonequivalent join nodes. But let's take a look at what happens when the clauses are not separate.

Listing 5-2 shows a seemingly innocuous variation on the rule shown in Listing 5-1. The only change is that the semicolons at the end of each of the first three conditions have been replaced with an "&&" "and" operation. The rule now has one condition that happens to have four sub-clauses. So what's the difference? Let's take a look at the `ACEPSTConditionsAnded` example.

Listing 5-2: *Fraud Rule with Conditions Anded*

```
rule Rules.Fraud {
  attribute {priority = 5; forwardChain = true; }
  declare {
    Events.Transaction transA;
    Events.Transaction transB;
  }
```

```
when {
  transB.transactionAmount <= 5.0 &&
  transA.transactionAmount >= 10000 &&
  transA.accountNumber == transB.accountNumber &&
  transA.transactionDateTime > transB.transactionDateTime ;
    /* C1 */
}
then {
  System.debugOut("Fraud!");
}
}
```

ACEPSTConditionsAnded Example

This example is identical to the ACEPSTConditionsSeparate example except for the fraud rule itself. But the Rete network that is created to evaluate the rule is quite different (Figure 5-16). In this network, after the type filter, there is only one node that evaluates the entire condition. Why is this bad? Take a look at what happens as transactions are introduced.

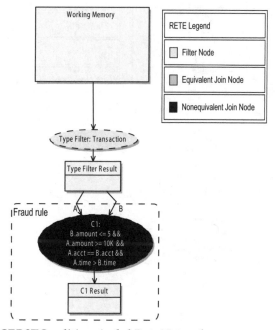

Figure 5-16: *ACEPSTConditionsAnded Rete Network*

Figure 5-17 shows the Rete network after T1 is introduced. Since T1 appears in the type filter result set, and this set is the only input to C1, the conditions of C1 are actually evaluated as the node attempts to join T1 with itself! Of course the join fails, but the computational resources were still expended.

Figure 5-18 shows the network after the introduction of T2. The appearance of T2 in the type filter result set triggers the evaluation of C1—three times! It will try to join T2 to itself and will try both combinations of T1 and T2. Only one of these combinations will produce the sought-after conclusion.

It is worth noting what happens as additional transactions are introduced into this network: Every possible combination of the transactions will be tried by C1. The computational complexity is thus n^2, where n is the number of transactions present in working memory. This isn't exactly the kind of computational complexity you want in your solutions.

As these two examples illustrate, the way in which you construct the conditional clauses in a rule has a significant impact on the amount of work done as the Rete network evaluates the rule conditions. The more you think about how the rule conditions are transformed into the Rete network for execution, the more efficient your solution will be.

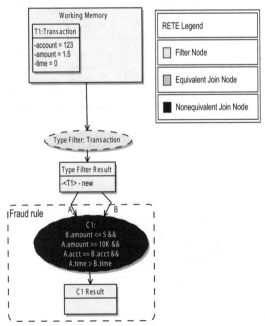

Figure 5-17: *ACEPSTConditionsAnded First Transaction Processing*

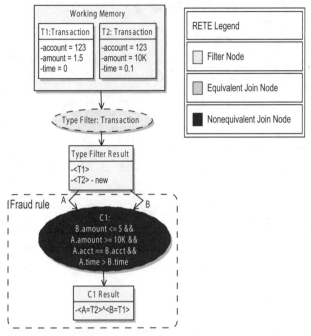

Figure 5-18: *ACEPSTConditionsAnded Second Transaction Processing*

Completing the Inference Agent: Preprocessing and Postprocessing

The RTC cycle operates on objects in the working memory, but we have not considered how those objects get there. This functionality is termed *pre-RTC processing* in the product manuals, or *preprocessing* for short (Figure 5-19). Preprocessing handles incoming communications. These communications usually (but not always) result in changes to working memory, which in turn trigger the evaluation of rules in the RTC cycle. The RTC processing takes actions that require outbound communications. The execution of these actions is termed *post-RTC processing*, or *postprocessing* for short.

There are three types of outbound communications, which occur only after the RTC processing is complete. One is the sending of events to other components and agents via channels. A second is the updating of objects in the cache: Objects that are configured to be in the cache and are created or modified by the inference agent must have their cache representations updated. The third is the updating of the cache

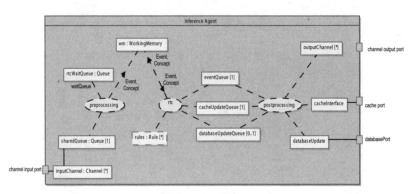

Figure 5-19: *Inference Agent Full View*

backing store if it is configured in a particular way (i.e., shared-all cache-aside). The cache update and backing store operations are detailed in Chapter 6.

Channels

Channels are the mechanism by which inference agents interact with external components and other TIBCO BusinessEvents agents. Numerous types of channels are available, including

- Java Message Service (JMS)
- TIBCO Rendezvous®
- HTTP
- TCP
- TIBCO ActiveSpaces®
- TIBCO Hawk®
- Local

The JMS and TIBCO Rendezvous channels provide the ability to send and receive messages. The HTTP and TCP channels enable the agent to play the role of both a server and a client with these protocols. The TIBCO ActiveSpaces channel lets the agent be a leach for an external space (not to be confused with the TIBCO BusinessEvents cache that happens to be implemented using the same technology). The TIBCO Hawk channel lets the agent interact with Hawk agents and Hawk-enabled components, providing access to component status and performance information. Lastly, the Local channel is available for interaction between agents co-located in the same processing unit. This channel is special in that the data structures being exchanged are not marshaled and unmarshaled (serialized and de-serialized) when this channel is being used: References to the parsed memory-resident data structures are simply handed from one agent to another.

Destinations

Each channel has one or more logical destinations associated with it (Figure 5-20). Non-local destinations have a default event type and a deserializer associated with them. When an incoming communication occurs, the deserializer creates an instance of the default event type populated with information from the incoming communication. Events created in this manner are automatically asserted into working memory.

In the outbound direction, each event type can have a default destination associated with it. When an event of that type is created and sent (`Event.sendEvent()`), it is sent to the default destination whose serializer creates the appropriate format for the outbound communication.

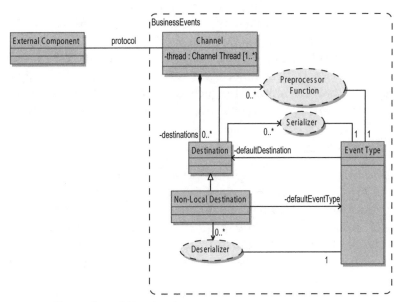

Figure 5-20: *Channels and Destinations*

Preprocessor Functions

Each destination has an option to designate a user-defined rule function as preprocessor function. This function must have one input parameter that is an event of a particular type.[4] When an event of that type is created by the destination, the preprocessor function associated with that event type is automatically called.

Preprocessor functions can be used to

- Modify the event (this is the only place where events may be edited)
- Consume the event (`Event.consumeEvent()`)
- Create new events
- Update working memory from cache (more about this in Chapter 6)
- Create concepts
- Update scorecards

A common modification of an event is to copy the information from selected fields in the payload data structure to properties of the event. The reason for doing this is efficiency: Properties are more efficiently accessed in rule conditions than fields in the payload.

Preprocessor functions can be used to filter events: Events that pass the filter conditions are asserted into working memory and further processed by rules. Those that do not pass the filter conditions are consumed. An alternative to filtering is to create a different type of event, often consuming the original event as well.

Rules related to the event often require other objects to be present in working memory. If these objects are not present, it is in the preprocessor function that the required objects are brought from the cache into the working memory or created initially. Scorecards can also be updated.

Directing Events

Events that are created in preprocessor functions and rule actions have no impact on execution until they are directed either to working memory or to a destination. Events are asserted into working memory with a call to the built-in function `Standard.Event.assertEvent()`. Events are sent to their default destination with `Standard.Event.sendEvent()`. An event can be sent as a reply to

---

4. This input parameter is designated by the scope section of the rule function.

an input with `Standard.Event.replyEvent()`. An Event can be sent to a destination other than its default destination with a call to `Standard.Event.routeTo(<destination>)`.

Preprocessing Behavior

The default preprocessing behavior is shown in Figure 5-21. An external event source generates a message, which is received by the channel and processed by the channel thread. The channel thread creates the event from the incoming message and places it on a shared queue.

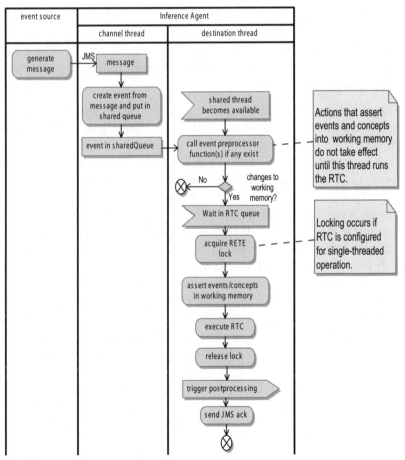

Figure 5-21: *Default Preprocessing Behavior*

The type of channel determines how many channel threads there are. For JMS, there is one. For HTTP, there is a pool of channel threads. You should consult the product manuals for details on the threads associated with each channel type.

Each destination designates the pool of threads that are used for preprocessing. There are three possibilities:

1. Shared Queue: This is the default. The event is placed in a queue shared by all destinations in this agent. There is a shared pool of threads for executing the preprocessor activities, and events wait in the shared queue until one of the threads from this pool becomes available.

2. Destination Queue: The event is placed in a queue specific to this destination. There is a pool of threads dedicated to this destination, and the event waits in the destination queue until one of these threads becomes available.

3. Caller Thread: There is no queue for this alternative. The channel thread (the one that created the event) immediately performs the preprocessor activities.

When a thread becomes available, if a preprocessor function has been associated with the event for this destination, it executes the function.

If the Concurrent RTC box in the inference agent configuration has not been checked (this is the default), then the thread is placed in a queue of threads waiting their turn to execute the RTC activities. If the box is checked, the thread immediately proceeds.

Once the thread is ready to execute, if the Concurrent RTC box is not checked the thread acquires the Rete lock. This prevents other threads from performing RTC activities. Any objects that were created or retrieved from the cache are asserted into working memory. Note that despite the fact that a call to `Event.assertEvent()` may have been made in the preprocessor function, the event is not actually placed in working memory until this point is reached. Once working memory has been updated, the RTC behavior (described earlier) is executed.

Upon completion of RTC, the lock is released (allowing other threads to execute RTC), a signal is sent to trigger the postprocessing related to the just-completed RTC, and (if necessary) the receipt of the initial JMS message is acknowledged. The thread is now ready to process another event.

Postprocessing Behavior

Once the RTC cycle has completed, there are a number of postprocessing activities to perform. Depending upon the value of the Boolean `Agent.<agentName>.enableParallelOps` property in the CDD file, these activities may be single-threaded or occur in parallel.

Figure 5-22 shows the behavior for the single-threaded option. If changes have been made to objects with the cache-aside object management option selected, the required database updates are performed first (this is further described in Chapter 6). Next the cache updates are performed. This sequencing ensures that object changes are not exposed in the cache until after the database operations have been successfully completed. Outbound events are sent next, followed by pending message acknowledgments. Finally, object locks are released (object locking is discussed in Chapter 6).

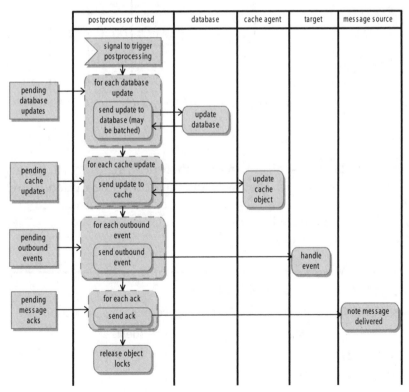

Figure 5-22: *Postprocessing Behavior—Single Threaded*

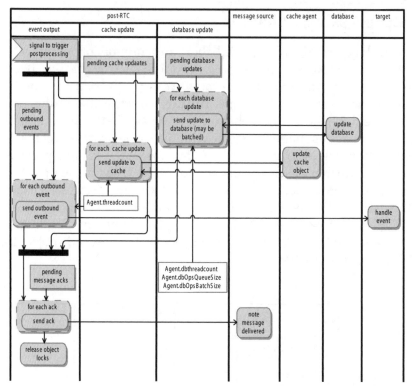

Figure 5-23: *Postprocessing Behavior—Multi-Threaded*

Figure 5-23 shows the behavior with multi-threading. All the activities run in parallel, with the event output and cache update activities using threads from the `Agent.threadcount` thread pool and the database update (if required) using threads from the `Agent.dbthreadcount` pool.

ACEPSTLocalChannel Example

The ACEPSTLocalChannel example illustrates several features, including

• Configuring a processing unit with two inference agents

• The use of local channels

• Rule actions publishing events

• Preprocessor functions creating and consuming events

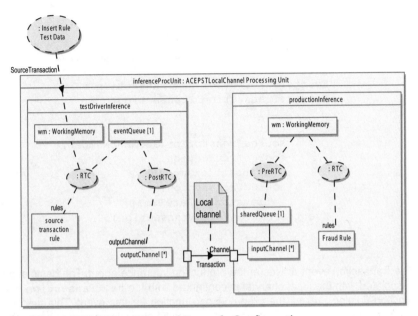

Figure 5-24: *ACEPSTLocalChannel Example Configuration*

Figure 5-24 shows the configuration of this example. It comprises a single processing unit named `inferenceProcUnit` that contains two inference agents: `testDriverInference` and `productionInference`. The two inference agents are configured with a local channel between them.

The test driver inference agent exists solely to feed transaction events to the production inference agent. When the example project is run in the debugger, the test data is fed directly into the working memory of the test driver inference agent. The test data comprises `SourceTransaction` events, which trigger the source transaction rule (Listing 5-3). The rule action creates a `Transaction` event using the data from the incoming event and sends the event to its default destination, which is associated with the local channel. This causes the newly created event to be sent to the production inference agent.

Listing 5-3: *Source Transaction Rule*

```
rule Rules.SourceTransaction {
      attribute {
            priority = 5;
            forwardChain = true;
      }
      declare {
            Events.SourceTransaction sourceTransaction;
      }
      when {
```

```
        }
        then {
              // Create the real transaction to drive
               the test
              Events.Transaction newTransaction =
              Events.Transaction.Transaction(
                    null,
                    null,
                    sourceTransaction.accountNumber,
                    sourceTransaction.
                       transactionAmount,
                    sourceTransaction.
                       transactionDateTime);
              Event.sendEvent(newTransaction);
        }
}
```

The Transaction event arrives at the production inference agent. The destination associated with the local channel is configured with the newTransaction rule function (Listing 5-4) as the preprocessor function for this event. This function takes the incoming transaction and determines whether its amount is below the $5 threshold or above the $10,000 threshold. If it is below the $5 threshold it creates and asserts a TinyTransaction, and if it is greater than $10,000 it creates and asserts GiantTransaction. In all cases, it consumes the original transaction.

Listing 5-4: *newTransaction Rule Function*

```
void rulefunction RuleFunctions.newTransaction {
      attribute {validity = ACTION;}
      scope {Events.Transaction transaction;  }
      body {
            if (transaction.transactionAmount <= 5.00) {
                  TinyTransaction tinyTransaction =
                       Events.TinyTransaction.TinyTransaction(
                        null,
                        null,
                        transaction.accountNumber,
                        transaction.transactionAmount,
                        transaction.transactionDateTime);
                  System.debugOut("Created tiny transaction:
                       " + tinyTransaction@id);
                  Event.assertEvent(tinyTransaction);
                  System.debugOut("Asserted tiny transaction:
                       " + tinyTransaction@id);
            }
            else if (transaction.transactionAmount >=
                  10000.00) {
                  GiantTransaction giantTransaction =
```

```
                      Events.GiantTransaction.
                          GiantTransaction(
                          null,
                          null,
                          transaction.accountNumber,
                          transaction.transactionAmount,
                          transaction.transactionDateTime);
                  System.debugOut("Created giant
                          transaction: " + giantTransaction@id);
                  Event.assertEvent(giantTransaction);
                  System.debugOut("Asserted giant
                          transaction: " + giantTransaction@id);
              }
              System.debugOut("About to consume transaction: " +
                      transaction@id);
              Event.consumeEvent(transaction);
              System.debugOut("Consumed transaction: " +
                      transaction@id);
          }
      }
```

This preprocessor function is doing two things: It is both classifying and filtering transactions. By classifying the transactions, it is making clear to the rule which transactions are below the lower threshold and which ones are above the large threshold. It is also filtering transactions: Any transaction between the two thresholds is simply consumed.

Asserting the tiny and giant transactions (which are configured with a time-to-live of one hour) triggers a new version of the Fraud Rule (Listing 5-5). This rule simply compares the account numbers and determines the order in which the transactions occurred. The determination as to whether each transaction was below the lower threshold or above the upper threshold was done in the preprocessor. Furthermore, the events will exist for only an hour, and thus the age of the transactions does not need to be determined.

Listing 5-5: *ACEPSTLocalChannel Fraud Rule*

```
rule Rules.Fraud {
      attribute {
            priority = 5;
            forwardChain = true;
      }
      declare {
            Events.GiantTransaction giantTransaction;
            Events.TinyTransaction tinyTransaction;
      }
      when {
            tinyTransaction.accountNumber ==
                  giantTransaction.accountNumber;
            giantTransaction.transactionDateTime >
```

```
                    tinyTransaction.transactionDateTime;
      }
      then {
            System.debugOut("Fraud!");
      }
}
```

State Models

The TIBCO BusinessEvents® Data Modeling extension adds the ability to define state machines and associate them with concepts. As shown in Figure 5-5, zero or more state machines (instances of state models) can be associated with a concept.

State Transitions

Each state machine has a start state, a number of intermediate states, and one or more end states (Figure 5-25). The state machine changes from one state to another via transitions. Each transition can have an associated rule. A transition without a rule is immediately taken as soon as the state at the beginning of the transition is taken. In this example, the absence of a rule on the transition between the Start state and State A indicates that as soon as the state machine is started it will enter State A.

A rule on a state machine transition is defined in a manner similar to other inference agent rules: The types of objects that trigger the rule are identified, conditions are defined, and actions are specified. The rule is triggered when the state at the beginning of the transition is entered. These rules are evaluated during the inference agent RTC cycle like normal rules with one exception: A transition rule can only fire once in an RTC cycle. Once all of its conditions have been met and the state transition has been taken, the rule will not fire again during that RTC cycle.

Figure 5-25: *State Machine Example*

Transition rules can have the same types of actions associated with them as regular inference agent rules. In addition, actions can be specified for execution when a state is entered and when the state is exited. One possible type of action is the starting or stopping of another state machine.

Timeouts

States can have timeouts associated with them. The timer starts when the state is entered. If the timer expires before the state is exited, the specified actions are taken and the state machine transitions to a specified state.

Despite the fact that the state machine starts the timer, the timer itself is not part of the state machine. Each timer is an object that is, by default, operated in cache-only mode and saved to the backing store (if so configured).

One of the inference agents in the cluster (determined automatically) operates a scheduler. The scheduler periodically checks the timers to see which have expired and executes the state machine logic associated with the timeout. Note that this timeout event does not go through a preprocessor, yet locking may still be required to safely execute the logic. To support this, state machine timeout callbacks can be registered that perform the same role as a preprocessor function. When locking (or other preprocessor functionality) is required for the timeout event, you must define and register the necessary function. The *TIBCO BusinessEvents Data Modeling Developer's Guide* provides the details.

Starting and Stopping State Machines

Each concept can have a main state machine associated with it. By default, this machine is configured to automatically start when the concept is created. By exception, the machine can be started using the catalog function `startStateMachine()`.

For more information on state machines, please consult the *TIBCO BusinessEvents Data Modeling Developer's Guide*.

Summary

An inference agent provides the ability to evaluate objects using rules. Each rule identifies the types of objects used by the rule, the conditions those objects must satisfy, and the actions to be taken when the conditions are met.

Inference agents operate on three key types of objects: events, concepts, and scorecards. An event is a representation of some external occurrence and is not modifiable except in the preprocessor function associated with its creation. Events are local to the agent that created them (with the exception of query agents) unless the event is explicitly sent via a channel.

Concepts are modifiable representations intended to be shared via the cache. They can be created in preprocessor functions and created, modified, and deleted in rule actions.

Scorecards are special types of concepts. For each type of scorecard there is exactly one instance of that scorecard in each inference agent using that scorecard. Scorecards are used to accumulate historical information within a processing agent.

Rules operate on objects in an inference agent's working memory. Newly created or modified objects in working memory trigger rules. The evaluation of rules occurs in the run-to-completion (RTC) cycle. The cycle begins by identifying all triggered rules and placing them in a list known as the rule agenda. The rule agenda is then sorted by the priority and rank of the rules. Then one rule is selected for evaluation and the Rete network required to evaluate its conditions is assembled. Objects from working memory are inserted into the Rete network one at a time, and the output of the Rete network is a collection of objects that have met the conditions. The actions of the rule are applied to these objects. Some of these actions may alter the contents of working memory.

When the evaluation of one rule has been completed, the rule agenda is again assembled. With forward chaining, changes in working memory may result in some of the rules that were in the agenda being removed, and others added. The agenda is sorted and a single rule is again evaluated. This process continues until there are no more rules in the agenda.

Channels provide the mechanisms for the inference agent to interact with external components and other agents. There are channels for JMS, TIBCO Rendezvous, HTTP, TCP, TIBCO ActiveSpaces, TIBCO

Hawk, and local channels for communicating between agents hosted in the same processing unit.

Channels have one or more destinations associated with them. For incoming events, each destination specifies the default type of event to be constructed and the deserializer to be used in its construction. The destination identifies an optional preprocessor function to be invoked after the event is created. Events may identify a default destination to which the event may be sent. The destination identifies the type of thread to be used for executing preprocessor activities.

Whatever thread performs the preprocessor activities associated with an event also executes the RTC cycle for that event. If the Concurrent RTC option is not selected, the thread must wait its turn before executing RTC. The use of the Concurrent RTC option requires the careful use of locking to avoid accidental interactions between threads executing RTC cycles.

Postprocessor activities consist of updating the cache (and cache-aside database) for cache-resident objects that have changed, sending outbound events, acknowledging the receipt of incoming messages, and releasing object locks that may have been obtained. Postprocessing may occur either single-threaded or multi-threaded.

Concepts can have state machines associated with them. A state machine consists of a number of states and transitions. Transitions can have rules associated with them that define the conditions under which the transition will be taken. Actions can be taken when rules fire and when states are entered or exited. Timeouts can be specified for individual states and the state machine as a whole. If the timer expires before the state is exited (or the machine reaches its end state), specified actions are taken and a specified state is entered.

Chapter 6

Cache Agents

Objectives

After reading this chapter you will be able to describe the roles of a cache and a cache agent. You will be able to explain how cache agents interact with inference engines and enable information sharing between inference agents. You will be able to describe how information in the cache can be persisted and made fault tolerant.

The Need for a Cache

Inference agents have a working memory, so why not just hold all of the information in working memory? Why is a cache needed?

There are several factors that contribute to the need for a cache.

- There is more information that can be reasonably held in one inference agent's working memory.

- There is more work than can one inference agent can handle, so the workload must be distributed across multiple agents, but the information must be available to all agents.

- There is information that is not relevant to the analysis of the current event. Its presence in working memory will cause unnecessary computation.

The Cache and Cache Agents

The TIBCO BusinessEvents® cache is a memory-resident repository of information that is managed by one or more cache agents (Figure 6-1). Cache agents must normally be deployed in different processing units than inference agents. An exception is available for development purposes: An anonymous cache agent may be deployed in an inference agent processing unit by checking the Enable Cache Storage box on the processing unit CDD configuration.

Object Management Modes

Simply adding a cache agent to a cluster does not automatically get objects into the cache. In order for the cache to be used, an appropriate object management mode must be selected. There are three object management modes available:

1. Cache Only
2. Memory Only
3. Cache + Memory

In the CDD configuration a default object management mode is selected for the cluster (Figure 6-2). By exception, alternate memory

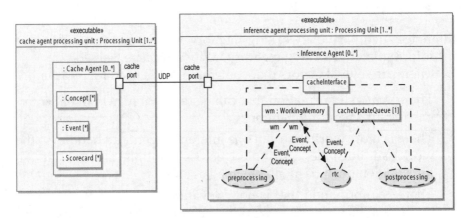

Figure 6-1: *Cache Agent Deployment*

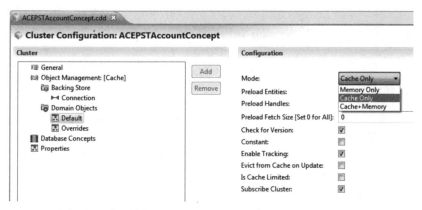

Figure 6-2: *Selecting the Object Management Mode*

management modes can be selected for individual object types or groups of types. The following sections describe the individual modes.

Cache Only

Cache only is the recommended default mode of operation. In this mode, objects reside in the cache and must be explicitly loaded into the inference agent's working memory by a preprocessor function.

When a cache-only object is brought into working memory, only its identifier is initially loaded. The data associated with the object is not loaded until it is actually accessed by the inference agent.

If a change is made to a cached object and that object happens to also be in working memory, the working memory copy of that object is updated, regardless of the state of the RTC processing. Locking (discussed later in this chapter) can be used to prevent this.

Cache-only objects are automatically removed from working memory at the end of the RTC cycle unless the Constant box is checked (this should only be done by exception—never for the default configuration). When this box is checked, once the object has been brought into working memory it will remain there until it is explicitly removed. These objects are typically loaded by start-up functions.

Memory Only

Objects configured with this mode reside only in working memory and do not appear in the cache. Such objects reside in exactly one inference agent.

The lifetime of objects using this mode depends upon the type of object. Concepts will remain until they are explicitly deleted. Events depend upon their time-to-live setting.

- Time-to-live = 0: The event will be deleted at the end of the RTC cycle.

- Time-to-live > 0: The event will be deleted after the specified time interval.

- Time-to-live < 0: The event will remain until explicitly deleted.

Cache + Memory

Objects configured with cache + memory mode reside both in the cache and in working memory. This mode should be used only for objects that do not change, as with static reference data. Any change to the object has wide-ranging performance implications since the change will possibly trigger every rule in every inference agent that uses the object type. To make matters worse, the triggering of all rules in all agents is not guaranteed. There are some additional restrictions that are discussed in the product manuals. Use this mode with caution.

ACEPSTAccountConcept Example

This example (Figure 6-3) illustrates both the use of concepts and the use of the cache. Since the example is intended to be run in the debugger and debugging is most convenient if a single processing unit is used, the processing unit has been configured to use an anonymous cache agent by selecting "Enable Cache Storage" in its CDD configuration file.

As with earlier examples, test data is inserted into the working memory of a testDriverInference agent, which generates transactions that are sent to the productionInferenceAgent via a local channel. Figure 6-4 shows the object types used in this example. There is a Transaction event along with Account and Transaction concepts.

An overview of the processing for this example is shown in Figure 6-5. When a Transaction event arrives, its amount is examined. If it is between the two thresholds, the event is discarded: It is not of interest.

If the transaction amount is below the small threshold or above the large threshold, an attempt is made to retrieve the related Account concept from the cache. Note that the concept may not exist. However, a successful retrieval will result in the account (and its contained tiny transaction, if it exists) being placed in working memory. Remember that placing a retrieved object into working memory will not trigger a rule!

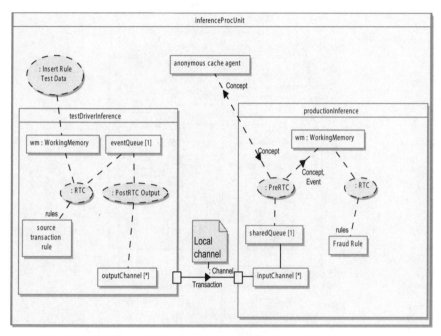

Figure 6-3: *ACEPSTAccountConcept Example Configuration*

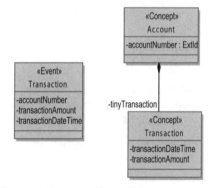

Figure 6-4: *ACEPSTAccountConcept Object Types*

If the transaction amount is larger than the small threshold (which means that it is also larger than the large threshold since all the transactions in between have been consumed at this point), it is simply asserted into working memory. The presence of this transaction event will trigger the evaluation of the fraud rule.

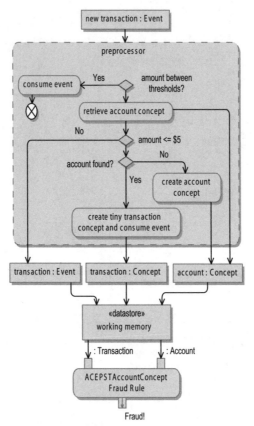

Figure 6-5: *ACEPSTAccountConcept Processing*

If the transaction amount is below the small threshold, the preprocessor will ensure that an `Account` concept exists (creating one if necessary) and will add a contained `Transaction` concept. However, the transaction event is consumed.

The fraud rule for this example is shown in Listing 6-1.

Listing 6-1: *ACEPSTAccountConcept Fraud Rule*

```
rule Rules.Fraud {
    attribute {
        priority = 5;
        forwardChain = true;
    }
    declare {
        Events.Transaction transaction;
        Concepts.Account account;
    }
    when {
```

```
            transaction.transactionAmount >= 10000;
            transaction.accountNumber ==
                Number.intValue(account@extId,10);
            // tiny transaction occurred within the past hour
            transaction.transactionDateTime <
                DateTime.addHour(
                    account.tinyTransaction.
                    transactionDateTime,1);
    }
    then {
            System.debugOut("Fraud!");
    }
}
```

Object Locking

If "Concurrent RTC" is enabled in an inference agent or there are multiple instances of an inference agent running the same set of rules, there is the potential for conflict as multiple rules access the same objects simultaneously. The purpose of object locking is to prevent such conflicts.

A lock in TIBCO BusinessEvents is a semaphore with a name that is referred to as a key. The key is just a string. You obtain a lock by calling the Lock function:

```
Cluster.DataGrid.Lock(<key>,<timeout>,<localOnly>)
```

The timeout specifies how long you will wait for the lock, and the <localOnly> Boolean indicates whether you only want to lock the copy of the object that happens to be in the inference agent obtaining the lock or whether you want the lock to be global.

The most important thing to realize about locks is that you are not locking an object. You are obtaining a lock on a string (the key). So how do you prevent access to the object? By following these programming conventions:

- Establish a convention for associating a key with an object. Typically the object's extID is used as the key.
- For editable objects, use the Lock function whenever the object is being accessed, regardless of whether it is a read or write operation you intend to perform.

The most common place to obtain a lock is in a preprocessor function. Locks are automatically released at the end of the RTC cycle.

If there are multiple objects that need to be locked, there is the possibility of a deadly embrace: X locks A and then tries to lock B, while Y has locked B and is attempting to lock A. Neither X or Y will be able to proceed. For this reason, it is important to specify the timeouts for the locks and provide appropriate exception handling.

The likelihood of a deadly embrace can be greatly reduced by following another programming convention: If you plan to lock multiple objects, then obtain all of their keys, sort the keys, and then obtain the locks in the sorted sequence.

Remember, the effectiveness of locks depends entirely upon the consistency of their use!

Cache Object Replication

The cache can be configured to automatically replicate objects, with the copies of objects residing in different cache agents (Figure 6-6). There are two settings for this configuration. One is Number of Backup Copies, which determines the number of extra copies (in addition to the original) that will be maintained in the cache. The default is one. The other setting is Cache Agent Quorum, which determines the minimum number of cache agents that must be running before the cluster will begin operating. It doesn't make any sense to have back-up copies of objects if they are all present in the same cache agent, so this number should be at least one greater than the number of back-up copies. If you want to maintain replication even if a cache agent goes down, increase this number. This setting has no effect on operation once the cluster has started other than causing a log entry to be made if the actual number of running cache agents falls below this number.

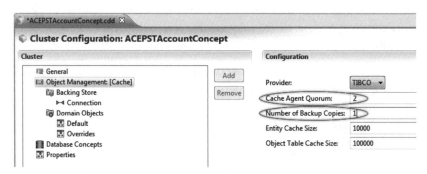

Figure 6-6: *Configuring Cache Object Replication*

Object Persistence

Object replication provides in-memory fault tolerance, but shutting down all of the cache agents (as would occur in a power failure) will still result in the loss of the information in the cache. Object persistence provides a way of preserving the information in the cache. There are three persistence options for a cluster (Figure 6-7):

1. None
2. Shared All (in a database)
3. Shared Nothing (in files)

Shared-All Option

Shared-All persistence saves the content of the cache in a database. When this option is selected, there are two additional choices to be made: the type of database to be used and whether the Cache-Aside update strategy will be used (Figure 6-8).

The available database options are

- Oracle
- SQL Server
- DB2
- Berkeley DB

The Cache-Aside option determines which type of agent will actually update the database. If the box is checked, the inference agent

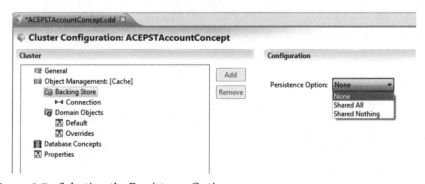

Figure 6-7: *Selecting the Persistence Option*

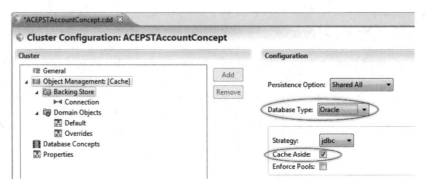

Figure 6-8: *Selecting Shared-All Options*

performs the database update. If the box is not checked, the cache agent performs the update. This is referred to as "Write Behind." Note that the Cache-Aside option is not available for the Berkeley DB.

Cache-Aside Behavior

With Cache-Aside, the inference agent performs the database update. This activity is performed in the postprocessing after the RTC cycle has completed. The details of this update are described in Chapter 5.

A key parameter driving this update is the `Agent.<agentName>.enableParallelOps` property in the CDD file for the agent that will be performing the update. Figure 5-22 shows the behavior when this property is set to `false`, and Figure 5-23 shows the behavior when the property is set to `true`.

When Cache-Aside is selected, database operations may be batched together and executed as a single transaction for efficiency. With `enableParallelOps = false`, all database updates occur before any cache updates.

Write-Behind Behavior

If the Cache Aside box is not checked, the result is Write-Behind behavior (Figure 6-9). In this mode, the inference agent updates the cache, and the cache agent, in turn, updates the database. In this mode, each individual cache object update results in a separate database transaction.

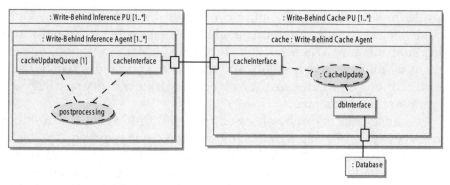

Figure 6-9: *Shared-All Write-Behind Configuration*

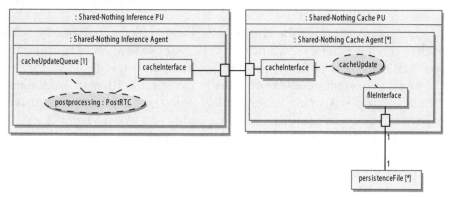

Figure 6-10: *Shared-Nothing Configuration*

Shared-Nothing Option

The Shared-Nothing option (Figure 6-10) is similar to the Shared-All Write-Behind option with two significant differences: cached objects are persisted in files instead of a database, and each cache agent has its own file. Because of these differences, the Shared-Nothing configuration will perform better than the Shared-All option. Furthermore, when combined with object replication, Shared-Nothing will record all replicated copies of the objects, thus providing fault tolerance for data even if one of the persistence files is lost or damaged.

Summary

The cache provides a means of sharing concepts between inference agents. There are three management modes for objects: Memory Only, Cache Only, and Cache + Memory. In Memory-Only mode, objects reside in working memory and never enter the cache. In Cache-Only mode, objects reside in the cache and must be explicitly brought into working memory when needed. In Cache + Memory mode, objects reside in both working memory and the cache. This mode must be used with caution, as any change to an object may trigger every rule in every agent that uses that object.

Because objects can be accessed from multiple agents or multiple threads within one agent, a locking mechanism is required. The locks provided by TIBCO BusinessEvents are logical: The objects themselves are not locked, key values are. A convention associates the key being locked with the object, with the common convention being the use of the object's `extID` as the lock key. Programming discipline is required to ensure the consistent use of locks.

The cache provides the ability to replicate objects in memory, with each copy of the object residing in a different cache agent. This guarantees that the object will survive the loss of a cache agent.

Objects in cache may be optionally persisted, either in a database (Shared-All option) or in files (Shared-Nothing option). With Shared-All, there are two sub-modes: Cache-Aside and Write-Behind. With Cache-Aside, the inference agent does the database update, while in Write-Behind the cache agent does the database update. In the Shared-Nothing option, each cache agent persists the objects in its memory to a separate file.

Chapter 7

Query Agents

Objectives

Query agents are part of the TIBCO BusinessEvents® Event Stream Processing product, an add-on to the core TIBCO BusinessEvents® product (Chapter 4).

After reading this chapter you will be able to describe the capabilities and appropriate uses for query agents and how snapshot and continuous queries work.

Snapshot Queries

A *snapshot query* is a query of the cache contents that is executed on-demand. The demand comes in the form of an event sent to a channel on the query agent (Figure 7-1).

Snapshot Query Execution

The processing associated with the query execution is split between the cache agent and the query agent (Figure 7-2). The cache agent performs filtering operations involving concepts in a manner similar to the inference agent's Rete network filters. Any objects that satisfy the filter

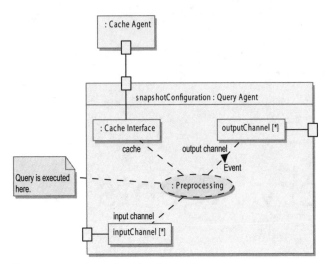

Figure 7-1: *Query Agent Snapshot Configuration*

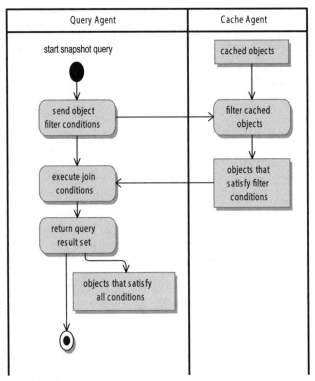

Figure 7-2: *Snapshot Query Execution*

conditions are forwarded to the query agent where joins are performed. Objects that pass all conditions are added to the query results.

An example query is shown in Listing 7-1. There is one where clause in the query, `accountNumber = $acctNo`. This is a filter condition: the `accountNumber` is compared against a variable whose value is fixed at the time the query is executed. The filter condition is passed to the cache agent, and the cache agent will return all accounts whose `accountNumber` matches the condition (hopefully only one!).

Listing 7-1: *Snapshot Query Example*

```
select account
from /Concepts/Account account
where accountNumber = $acctNo
```

The query agent can query all of the contents of the cache. In addition to concepts, this may include events and scorecards present in the cache, even though they are otherwise inaccessible to other agents.

Snapshot Query Life Cycle

The configuration and execution of a snapshot query is done by executing code (Figure 7-3). The first step in the process is to create (define) the query using the `Query.create()` function. The function parameters are the name you choose for the query and a string containing the query definition (Listing 7-1 is an example of such a string). The query definition is parsed, and the function will throw an exception if there is an error in the query definition.

There are two places you might put the query creation code: in a rule function that is designated as a start-up function or in the preprocessor function that will eventually execute the query. If the query definition will not change, the start-up function is a good choice: The process of parsing the query definition will occur only once. But if the query definition depends upon the current context, it will have to go in the preprocessor function.

Once the query has been created, the next step is to create an instance of the query using the `Query.Statement.open()` function. Creating instances of the query allows multiple queries of the same type to be executed concurrently. If there are variables in the query (e.g., `$acctNo` in Listing 7-1), the third step is to set the values of these variables using the `Query.Statement.setVar()` function.

The query is actually executed with the `Query.Statement.execute()` function. An argument to this function is the identifier

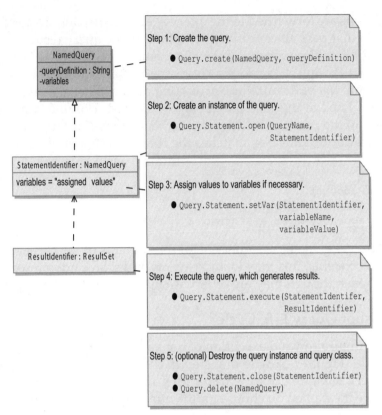

Figure 7-3: *Snapshot Query Life Cycle*

that you want to assign to the `ResultsSet` data structure that will be returned. Once the query has executed, you can use the `Query` `.ResultsSet.xxx` functions to examine the contents of the results set.

Optionally, you can close the statement and delete the query if desired.

ACEPSTSnapshotQuery Example

Figure 7-4 shows the configuration of this example.

When the `InferenceQueryPU` is started, it executes the start-up function in Listing 7-2. This start-up function creates the `FraudQuery`.

Listing 7-2: *ACEPSTSnapshotQuery Query Agent Start-up Function*

```
void rulefunction RuleFunctions.queryStartup {
  attribute {
    validity = ACTION;
  }
  scope {
```

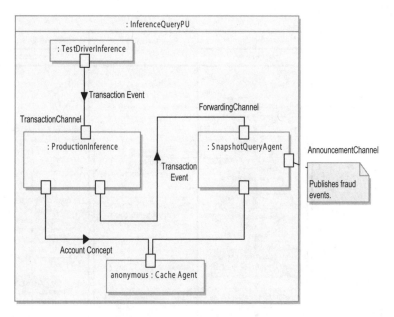

Figure 7-4: *ACEPSTSnapshotQuery Configuration*

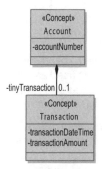

Figure 7-5: *Concepts Used in ACEPSTSnapshotQuery*

```
  }
  body {
    Query.create("FraudQuery","select account from/Concepts/
      Account account where accountNumber = $acctNo");
  }
}
```

The Account concept and associated tinyTransaction Transaction concept used in the example in Listing 7-2 are shown in Figure 7-5.

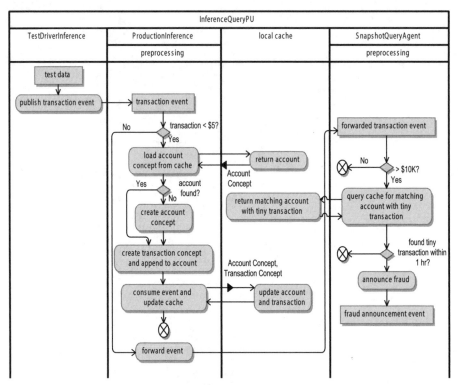

Figure 7-6: *ACEPSTSnapshotQuery Behavior*

An overview of this example's behavior is shown in Figure 7-6. The `TestDriverInference` agent is used as the insertion point for test data. A rule in this agent generates a `Transaction` event, which is sent to the `ProductionInference` inference agent.

The `ProductionInference` agent has a preprocessor function associated with this event. The function first checks to see whether the amount exceeds the small threshold. If it does, it forwards the transaction to the query agent. It if does not, it attempts to retrieve the `Account` concept from the cache, and if one is not found, it creates it. Next, it appends a `Transaction` concept as the `Account. tinyTransaction`, consumes the event, and allows the cache to be updated.

The preprocessor in the `SnapshotQueryAgent` checks the transaction to see whether it exceeds the large threshold. If it does, it queries the cache to see if there has been a tiny transaction within the past hour. If one is found, it announces the fraud.

The preprocessor function for the `SnapshotQueryAgent` is shown in Listing 7-3. It synthesizes unique identifiers for both the statement and the result set. It opens the statement (i.e., creates an instance of the query) and sets the value of the `acctNo` variable. It executes the query and examines the results to see if there is an account with a tiny transaction that occurred within the past hour. If one is found, it makes an announcement both with a `System.debugOut( )` statement and the sending of a `fraudEvent`.

Listing 7-3: *ACEPSTSnapshotQuery Query Agent Preprocessor Function*

```
void rulefunction RuleFunctions.recognizeFraudWithQuery {
attribute {validity = ACTION;}
scope {
  Events.Transaction transaction;
}
body {
  // We must create a unique identifier for this
  // instance of the query and for the result set
  if (transaction.transactionAmount >= 10000) {
    String id = String.valueOfInt(transaction@id);
    String statementId = "S" + id;
    String resultSetId = "R" + id;
    Query.Statement.open("FraudQuery",statementId);
    Query.Statement.setVar(statementId,
        "acctNo", transaction.accountNumber);
    Query.Statement.execute(statementId,resultSetId);
    while (Query.ResultSet.next(resultSetId)){
      Concepts.Account account = Query.ResultSet.
      get(resultSetId,1);
      // If the large transaction is within an hour
      // of the account's tiny transaction,
      // announce that we have fraud.
      if (transaction.transactionDateTime < DateTime.addHour(
          account.tinyTransaction.transactionDateTime,1)) {
        System.debugOut("Fraud on account number: " +
          String.valueOfInt(transaction.accountNumber));
        Events.FraudAnnouncement fraudEvent =
          Events.FraudAnnouncement.FraudAnnouncement(
              null,null,transaction.accountNumber);
        Event.sendEvent(fraudEvent);
      }
    }
  }
}
}
```

Continuous Queries

A continuous query operates on a buffer of objects that is located in the query agent. The buffer is fed from two possible sources: cache agents and channels.

The `from` clause of the query specifies the types of objects that are of interest and the policy for their retention in the buffer. In Listing 7-4, this clause indicates that `GiantTransaction` and

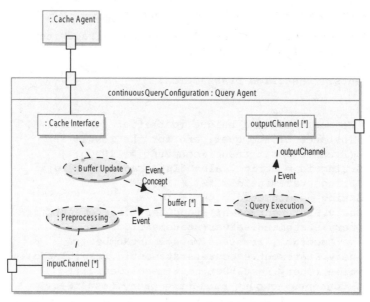

Figure 7-7: *Query Agent Continuous Query Configuration*

`TinyTransaction` events are of interest, new events should be added, and they should be retained in the buffer for one hour. The `where` clause is reevaluated whenever the buffer contents change.

Listing 7-4: *Continuous Query Example*

```
select
  giantTransaction.accountNumber
from
  /Events/GiantTransaction {
     policy: maintain last 1 hours;
     accept:new} giantTransaction,
  /Events/TinyTransaction {
     policy:maintain last 1 hours;
     accept:new} tinyTransaction
where
     giantTransaction.accountNumber = tinyTransaction.
        accountNumber and
     giantTransaction.transactionDateTime >
       tinyTransaction.transactionDateTime");
```

Buffer Management

The logic for determining the buffer content is defined in the `from` clause of the query. There are two management strategies: explicit and implicit.

Explicit

In *explicit buffer management* a policy clause defines the conditions under which the object will be added and the logic defining its retention. Listing 7-4 indicates that new objects will be accepted (added), and that the objects will be retained for one hour. There are three types of retention policy available.

1. Sliding: The last n objects meeting specified conditions will be retained.

2. Tumbling: Retains up to n objects, at which point the buffer is emptied to start over.

3. Time window: Objects remain in the buffer for the specified time period.

Listing 7-4 has two examples of explicit buffer management using time windows.

Implicit

In *implicit buffer management*, there is no policy clause in the query. New objects that meet the specified conditions are added to the buffer and deleted objects are removed. Changed objects are first removed from the buffer (without triggering the query evaluation) and then added (which will trigger the query evaluation).

Continuous Query Life Cycle

The life cycle of a continuous query is shown in Figure 7-8. The cycle begins with a call to `Query.create()`. One of the arguments to this function is the string that defines the query. Note that this function may throw an exception if there is an error in the query definition.

Once the query has been created, an instance of the query is created with `Query.Statement.open()` and the values of variables set with calls to `Query.Statement.setVar()`. Executing the query with `Query.Statement.execute()` requires a user-defined callback function. This is a user-defined rule function that must have the type signature required for query statement callbacks. The body of the function contains the logic indicating what to do with the query results. The function is called each time the query is reevaluated.

Once executed, the query remains active until the agent is shut down or `Query.Statement.close()` is called.

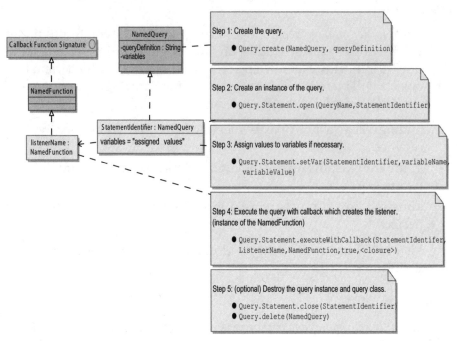

Figure 7-8: *Continuous Query Life Cycle*

It is common practice to create the query in a start-up function that runs when the agent is started. If you want the query to always be active, the instance can be created and executed here as well. If you only want the query to be active some of the time, define events to trigger the starting and stopping of the query, and use preprocessor functions for these events to invoke the requisite functions.

ACEPSTContinuousQuery Example

The ACEPSTContinuousQuery example (Figure 7-9) involves three agents. The TestDriverInference agent takes the test data and generates a Transaction event, which is sent to the ProductionInference agent. The ProductionInference agent screens these transactions and generates instances of TinyTransaction and GiantTransaction, which are sent to the queryAgent.

Figure 7-10 shows the execution details for this example. The Production-Inference agent examines the incoming Transaction and generates a TinyTransaction if the amount is less than $5, and it generates a GiantTransaction if the amount is greater than $10,000. It then consumes the Transaction. The generated transactions are sent to the queryAgent.

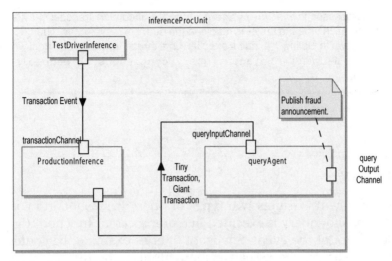

Figure 7-9: *ACEPSTContinuousQuery Configuration*

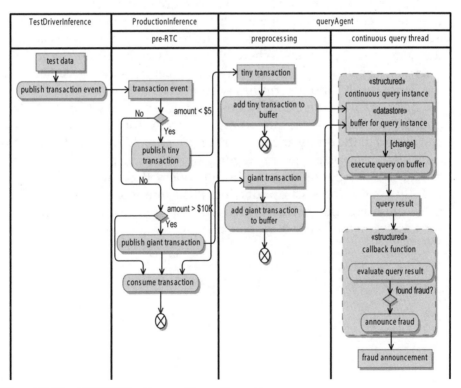

Figure 7-10: *ACEPSTContinuousQuery Execution*

The preprocessor in the `queryAgent` adds the incoming transactions to the buffer, and each time the buffer is modified the query is reevaluated. The query is the one shown in Listing 7-4, and it executes in a thread from a thread pool whose size can be set with the `be.agent.query.continuous.threadpoolsize` parameter.

Summary

The query agent executes two types of query: snapshot and continuous. A snapshot query is executed in a preprocessor function triggered by the receipt of the event. Snapshot queries examine the contents of the cache. The preprocessor function running the query determines what to do with the query results, either sending the results in the form of an event or analyzing the results and taking appropriate actions.

Continuous queries operate on a buffer of objects. The query specifies the types of objects in the buffer along with the conditions for their addition and removal. The objects can come from either the cache or the query agent channels. When the contents of the buffer change, the query is reevaluated. A user-defined callback function is called with the query results and determines what actions to take.

Both snapshot and continuous queries are defined, instantiated, and executed by invoking functions. Typically, the query definition is performed in the query agent's start-up function. The instantiation and execution of snapshot queries is generally done in a preprocessor function. The instantiation of a continuous query that runs all the time is usually done in the start-up function. If the query only runs part of the time, these functions will be invoked in preprocessor functions that start and stop the query in response to incoming events.

Chapter 8

Process Agents

Objectives

This chapter covers the operation of the process agent. After reading this chapter you will be able to describe the intended utilization of the process agent, how processes are defined, the available types of process tasks, and how processes execute. You will also be able to explain process checkpointing and recovery, as well as some restrictions on process agent deployment.

Intended Utilization

While rules provide a very powerful paradigm for analyzing situations and drawing conclusions, there are some things that are actually difficult to do with rules. One of these is to orchestrate the execution of multiple activities being performed by other components, particularly when some of the activities involve asynchronous interactions. The purpose of the process agent is to provide a convenient means for implementing this type of process orchestration.

One common application of the process agent is to provide an orchestrated response to an event (Figure 8-1). In this type of application, some other component (e.g., an inference agent) has announced the existence of a situation that requires an orchestrated response. In this example, the recognition of potential fraud resulted in the generation

127

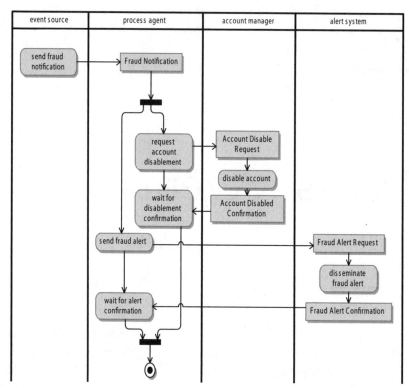

Figure 8-1: *Orchestrated Actions Example*

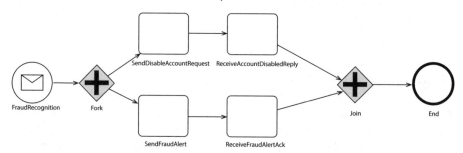

Figure 8-2: *Process Agent Design for Orchestrated Actions*

of a fraud notification. The required response is to disable the account and send a fraud alert. The nature of the account manager and alert system requires that these interactions be asynchronous. The process agent sends both of these requests and then waits for their corresponding acknowledgments before terminating its process.

Figure 8-2 shows the process agent design for this example.

Another application is one in which the analysis requires orchestration. In the example of Figure 8-3, transactions are initially classified to

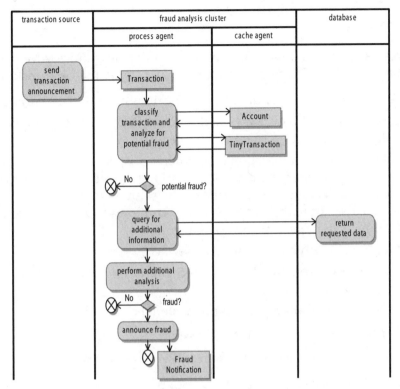

Figure 8-3: *Orchestrated Analysis*

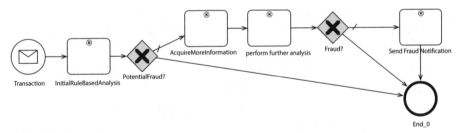

Figure 8-4: *Implementation of Orchestrated Analysis*

recognize `TinyTransactions` and `GiantTransactions` as was done in the previous chapter. These classified transactions are then analyzed to determine whether there is potential fraud. If there is, then additional information is retrieved from a database and a further analysis conducted to reach a final conclusion as to whether there is actually fraud.

The process agent configuration for this analysis is shown in Figure 8-4.

Processes

Processes are defined using a subset of the Business Process Modeling Notation (BPMN). There are a number of task types available, including

- Script: Executes a standard TIBCO BusinessEvents® rule function
- Business Rule: Invokes a virtual function whose implementation is a decision table (described in Chapter 10)
- Inference: The RTC portion of an inference agent embedded within the process. Operates against a working memory in the process agent and specifies a set of rules to be evaluated when the activity is invoked. The working memory is common to all processes and all inference tasks in the process agent.
- Web Service: Invokes an external service
- Sub-Process: An embedded BPMN diagram that is executed when the activity is invoked
- Call Activity: Calls a process that is defined elsewhere
- Message: Sends or receives a message

Each process has a starter activity. There are four types of starters:

1. Message Start: Creates an instance of the process when an event of the specified type arrives at a channel's queue-based destination. The event is consumed.
2. Signal Start: Creates an instance of the process when an event of the specified type arrives at a channel's topic-based destination. The event is not consumed.
3. Timer Start: Creates an instance of the process when a TIBCO BusinessEvents Timer Event is generated.
4. Start: An instance of the process is created either when another process executes a Call activity or when the process is designated as a start-up or shutdown process for the process agent.

Behavior

The behavior of the process agent is shown in Figure 8-5. The arrival of an event whose type is associated with a process causes the agent's preprocessor to create an instance of the process. Tasks that are ready to be executed are then placed on the task queue.

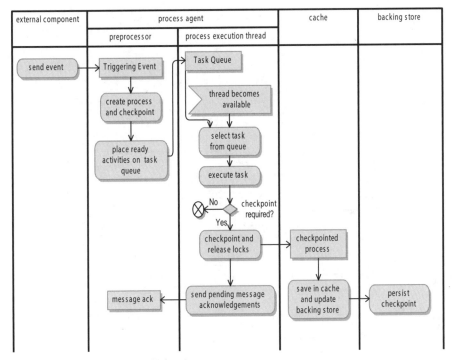

Figure 8-5: *Process Agent Behavior*

When a process execution thread becomes available, it takes one task from the head of the queue and executes it. If the task implicitly requires a checkpoint or has the checkpoint box checked, the process is checkpointed to the cache and, if configured, the backing store as well. Any object locks that have been acquired are released, and any pending message receipt acknowledgments are sent.

A *checkpoint* is the full state of the process at the moment the checkpoint is taken. It contains the state of the process's execution and the values of all variables associated with the process. Processes are managed using the cache-only approach (described in Chapter 6), and checkpointing is the update of the cached copy.

A checkpoint is performed whenever any of the following conditions occurs.

- A task is performed that has its Checkpoint box checked
- A Send Message task is executed
- A Receive Message task is executed
- A Call Activity is executed
- A Gateway task is executed (a fork, join, or conditional branch)
- A process ends

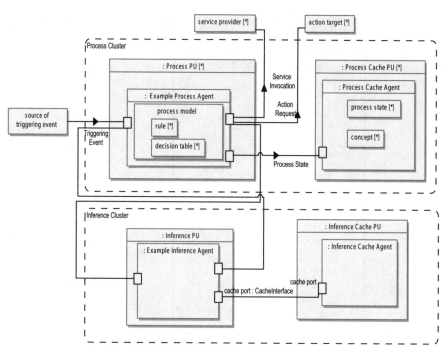

Figure 8-6: *Process Agent Deployment*

It is important to note that whenever a checkpoint occurs, all locks that the process has obtained are released.

Should a process agent fail or be shut down before a checkpointed process finishes executing, the process will be recovered by the next process agent that starts.

Deployment

Due to potential conflicts in cached object identities, process agents cannot be deployed in the same cluster as inference agents (Figure 8-6). Thus a solution requiring both inference and processing agents would require a separate cluster for each, with each cluster having its own cache agents.

Summary

Process agents provide the ability to orchestrate tasks, including those that require asynchronous interactions. The processes executed by the agent are defined using a subset of the industry-standard BPMN notation.

Each process has a starter task. Some starter tasks identify a type of event whose occurrence will cause the creation of a process instance. Processes without such tasks are explicitly invoked either with a Call Activity from another process or as a start-up or shutdown activity for a process agent.

Once a process has been started, its tasks that are ready to run are placed on a queue. When a process execution thread becomes available, it takes a task off the queue and executes the activity.

Processes are managed as cached objects. Certain tasks in the process initiate checkpoints that update the cache. Any locks that have been obtained by the process are released when a checkpoint occurs. Should a process agent be shut down or fail before a checkpointed process completes, the next process agent that starts will recover any incomplete processes.

Process agents cannot be deployed in the same cluster as an inference agent.

Chapter 9

Dashboard Agents

Objectives

The dashboard agent provides capabilities for the real-time visualization of information in both graphical and tabular form. After reading this chapter you will be able to describe the capabilities and appropriate uses of the dashboard agent.

Dashboard Configuration

The dashboard agent is used to provide real-time displays of information in a browser (Figure 9-1). The agent displays metric information that is created by an inference agent. The metric information is derived from information present in incoming events. A typical configuration involves several processing units, with inference, cache, and dashboard agents each deployed in dedicated processing units.

Processing units used for TIBCO BusinessEvents® Views use a special executable: `be-views.exe`. This is a standard executable extended to include the interfaces necessary to interact with the browser for dashboard display.

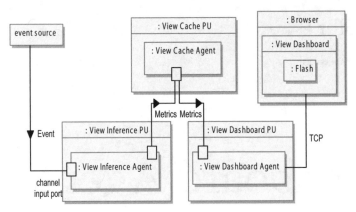

Figure 9-1: *View Configuration*

Behavior

The overall behavior of TIBCO BusinessEvents Views is shown in Figure 9-2. An external component sends an event that an inference agent is monitoring. The inference agent examines the event, extracts relevant information, and populates a special kind of object known as a metric (described in the next section). The metric, configured in cache-only mode, ends up in the cache. The dashboard agent, which is configured to display that type of metric, is notified by the cache that a metric has been updated. The dashboard agent determines the updates to the graphs, and charts and triggers their redisplay in the browser.

Metrics

A *metric* is a type of TIBCO BusinessEvents® object used to accumulate information for display (Figure 9-3). The metric type has two classes of fields: metric fields and tracking fields. Metric fields provide the data for the graphical displays and come in two varieties, aggregation fields and group-by fields. Aggregation fields provide the numeric data used in charts and graphs, while group-by fields define the categories for the data. Tracking fields are used to associate auxiliary data such as web site URLs with metric data. These fields can be displayed in charts.

Metrics can aggregate data in a number of ways, accumulating a set of raw data or computing the min, max, count, sum, average, standard deviation, or variance of the data.

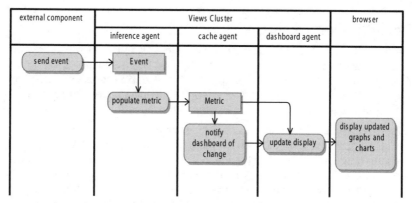

Figure 9-2: *TIBCO BusinessEvents® Views Behavior*

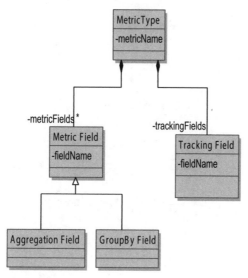

Figure 9-3: *Metric Meta-Data*

Dashboard

Accumulated metric data can be displayed in either tabular or graphical form in a web browser. Each chart or graph defines a query that selects the metrics to be displayed. Formatting information is provided at design time. Visual alerts can be configured as well, specifying the threshold at which the alert is triggered and the visual characteristics to be used in visualizing the alert.

TickerTracker Example

The TickerTracker example, distributed with the TIBCO BusinessEvents Views product, illustrates the use of metrics and the dashboard agent by showing how stock market information might be displayed. The example listens to Ticker events (Figure 9-4), which contain the ticker symbol, the trading price of the shares, the number of shares traded, and the full company name.

The preprocessor of the inference agent receives this event and updates the `M_TickerTracker` metric shown in Figure 9-5. The `Price` and `Volume` metric fields are aggregation fields, with each incoming price and volume being added. The `Ticker`, which is the stock market ticker symbol, is a group-by field: the `Price` and `Volume` are grouped by the ticker symbol with which they are associated. Finally, the `CompanyName` is a tracking field that has a URL providing a link to company information.

The resulting dashboard display is shown in Figure 9-6. The latest price and volume information are shown in both the table and the graph.

Clicking on any row of the table or column in the graph will bring up a display of the complete metric, showing the full set of price and volume data associated with the metric (Figure 9-7).

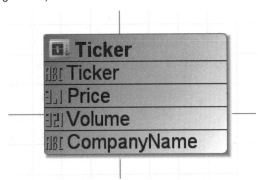

Figure 9-4: *TickerTracker Ticker Event*

M_TickerTracker.metric

Metric: M_TickerTracker

▾ Configuration

Description

▾ Metric Fields

✛ Add ✖ Remove ⊞ Fit Content

Name	Group By	Aggregation Type	Auxiliary Fields	Data Type	URL Name	URL Link	Description
Ticker	☑			String	Financial Info	http://finance.yahoo.com/q?s=$...	
Price	☐	Set		double			
Volume	☐	Set		long			

▾ Tracking Fields

✛ Add ✖ Remove ⊞ Fit Content

Name	Data Type	URL Name	URL Link	Description
CompanyName	String	Company Info	/page.html?stoken=${USR:TOKEN}$pagetype...	

Figure 9-5: *M_TickerTracker Metric Definition*

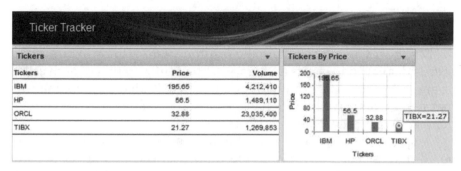

Figure 9-6: *Dashboard Display*

Figure 9-7: *M_TickerTracker Drill Down*

Deployment

If metric information changes frequently, considerable resources may be required to maintain the real-time display of the dashboard. For this reason, it is recommended that the entire set of agents used to maintain the view be executed in a cluster that is separate from the solution whose information is being displayed. Communications between the two clusters can use JMS as a transport. The cluster managing the views should be run on different machines than the solution cluster to avoid resource conflicts.

It is good practice to run the inference and dashboard agents in different processing units. Since their resource demands will likely grow at different rates, this will allow them to be tuned independently.

Summary

TIBCO BusinessEvents Views provides a means of maintaining a real-time display of solution information. Data is accumulated in metric objects that are created and updated by inference agents. The resulting metrics reside in the cache.

Dashboard agents maintain the real-time data display in browsers. Data is displayed in charts and graphs. The configuration of each chart or graph includes the definition of a query that identifies the metrics that will be displayed. Optionally, charts and graphs may be configured to display visual alerts.

A special executable is used for processing units running dashboard agents. For best results, the inference, cache, and dashboard agents being used for maintaining a dashboard should be deployed in a cluster that is separate from the cluster used for the solution being monitored. Preferably this cluster should be deployed on different machines as well. This will prevent resource demand conflicts between the solution and the dashboard.

Part III

Design Patterns

Chapter 10

Solution Basics

Objectives

This chapter focuses on basic capabilities you will require in crafting your solutions using TIBCO BusinessEvents®. After reading this chapter you will be able to

- Describe the various ways in which a change in a situation can be recognized and acted upon
- Describe how the sequencing or conditional execution of actions can be managed
- Describe how rules can be modified at runtime without halting your solution
- Explain the options available for exception reporting and logging
- Explain the naming guidelines for rules and rule functions

Recognizing a Situation Change

Central to complex-event processing solutions is the recognition of a situation that requires action. Often this requires not just the recognition that a situation has arisen, but also a deeper understanding of how the situation has changed. Typically this recognition of change then becomes the trigger for further analysis.

This chapter presents several common design patterns for recognizing a situation change:

- Reference-Data Comparison pattern
- Reference-Data Change pattern
- State Machine Change Recognition pattern
- Continuous Query Change Recognition pattern

Reference-Data Comparison Pattern

One approach to recognizing change is to compare current status against reference data (Figure 10-1). For example, a patient's current blood pressure is compared against an earlier reading to determine whether there has been a significant change.

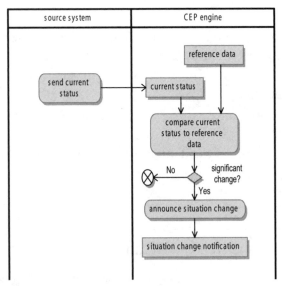

Figure 10-1: *Reference-Data Comparison Pattern*

Systems of Record for Reference Data

The reference data used in the Reference-Data Comparison pattern is generally historical data. The dominant design problem that arises in this pattern is that of maintaining the historical data. In crafting your solution, you need to answer three questions:

1. What is the system of record for the reference data?
2. How is the system of record being updated when the reference data changes?
3. How is the reference data made available to the CEP engine?

   There are several possible approaches.

TIBCO BusinessEvents® as Reference-Data System of Record

When you are using TIBCO BusinessEvents, answering the first question boils down to whether you want TIBCO BusinessEvents to be the system of record or some other system. If TIBCO BusinessEvents is to be the system of record, you're going to end up with a pattern similar to that of Figure 10-2 for maintaining the reference data. Here the inference agent has a rule that updates the cache, which in turn updates the backing store. This is the pattern you get if you use the shared-nothing option or shared-all with write-behind option discussed in Chapter 6.

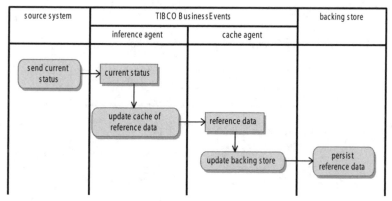

Figure 10-2: *TIBCO BusinessEvents® as Reference-Data System of Record*

Database as Reference-Data System of Record

Another alternative is to use a database as the system of record (Figure 10-3). The TIBCO BusinessEvents® Data Modeling extension provides the facilities for automatically defining the cached concept representation of the reference data based on the database schema and the operations for updating the database and updating the cache from the database. This pattern makes the reference data available to other systems as well.

External System as Reference-Data System of Record

A third alternative is to use an external system as the system of record for the reference data. A seemingly simple approach is shown in Figure 10-4, but there is a drawback: If some other entity changes the data in the external system, there is no mechanism for getting the change back into the cache.

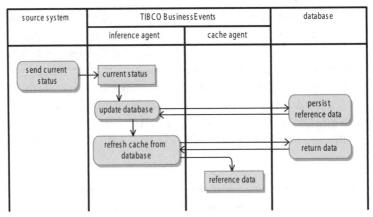

Figure 10-3: *Database as Reference-Data System of Record*

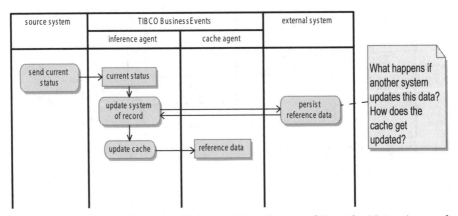

Figure 10-4: *External System as Reference-Data System of Record—Naïve Approach*

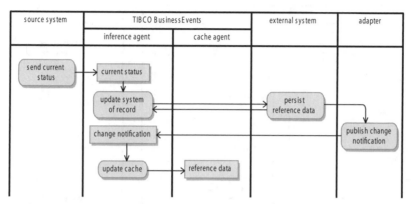

Figure 10-5: *External System as Reference-Data System of Record—Robust Approach*

A more robust approach is shown in Figure 10-5. Here the inference agent updates the system of record, and an adapter (such as the TIBCO ActiveMatrix® Adapter for Database) recognizes the change and publishes a change notification. The inference agent picks up this change notification through a channel and updates the reference data accordingly.

Reference-Data Change Coordination Patterns

The activities of comparing status to reference data and updating the reference data must be somehow coordinated. In a rule-based system, the simplest approach to performing these activities is to use separate rules for each activity (Figure 10-6a). This approach has a race condition and cannot guarantee that the comparison will finish (or even begin) before the reference data update occurs.

A more robust approach is to coordinate these two activities to ensure that the comparison completes before the update begins (Figure 10-6b). TIBCO BusinessEvents provides three mechanisms that can be used to ensure this sequencing.

1. Leave the two activities as separate rules and use rule priorities to ensure the proper sequence of execution (this is discussed later in this chapter).

2. Have a single rule that performs the two activities sequentially in the action part of the rule.

3. Use process orchestration as described in Chapter 8.

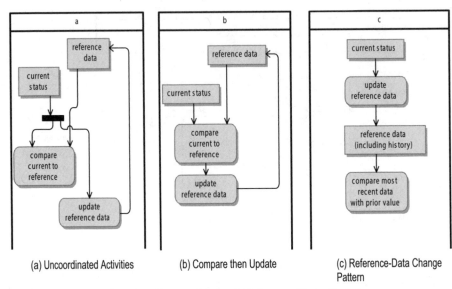

(a) Uncoordinated Activities   (b) Compare then Update   (c) Reference-Data Change Pattern

Figure 10-6: *Coordinating Comparison and Reference-Data Update*

Yet another approach is the Reference-Data Change pattern: Update the reference data first and let the reference data update drive the comparison (Figure 10-6c). This approach requires that the reference data maintain some historical data so that the triggered analysis has both the current and prior values available. In TIBCO BusinessEvents, concept properties have a configuration option that maintains historical values (see Chapter 5). Using this capability, there are three mechanisms that will provide the required sequencing.

1. Update the reference data in the cache and have a rule triggered by the change to the reference data that performs the comparison (see the sidebar).

2. Update the reference data in an external system (the system of record) and use an adapter to generate a change notification event (as was done in Figure 10-5) whose arrival triggers the comparison.

3. Use process orchestration to perform the update and then perform the comparison.

Recognizing Changes to Cached Objects

When using TIBCO BusinessEvents to update a cached object and having that change trigger the execution of a rule, bear in mind that most objects are managed in cache-only mode: The object will not be present in an inference agent unless some preprocessor logic has explicitly brought the object into the agent's working memory. The typical sequence is that the arrival of an event triggers a rule that updates the object: The preprocessor for that event will bring the cached object into working memory.

In order for a rule to be subsequently triggered by a change to that object, this rule must be deployed in the same inference agent as the rule that made the change to the object. If rules are split up and deployed to different inference agents (as is frequently done in complex applications), you must bear in mind that rules triggered by the change in an object must be deployed to the same agent as the rules that modify the object when you decide which rules to deploy to which inference agents.

Note that this consideration applies to all types of objects: events, concepts (including those with associated state machines), scorecards, processes, and metrics. If you have an inference agent rule triggered by an object change, that rule must be deployed in the same inference agent that made the change to the object.

State Machine Change Recognition Pattern

When the situation you are monitoring is modeled with a state machine, the machine itself can be used to announce changes in the situation (Figure 10-7). Transitions can be configured to send notifications. For example, the transition from `Start` to `State X`, which is taken when `Event 1` occurs, can be configured to send `Notification A` when the transition is taken. States can also be configured to send notifications when they are entered or exited. For example, `State X` is configured to send `Notification B` when it is entered and `Notification C` when it is exited.

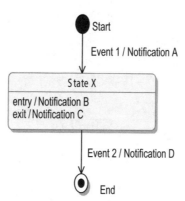

Figure 10-7: *State Machine Change Recognition Pattern*

A more realistic example is the sales order life cycle of Figure 10-8. Here the challenge is to notify accounting when the sales order has been fully delivered so that the revenue can be recognized from the sale. Since partial shipments are possible, recognizing that the order has been fully delivered is potentially complex, hence the use of the state machine to track the situation. Note the conditions on the transitions for `Shipping Notice` and `Delivery Notice` events, checking to see whether the order has been partially or fully shipped or delivered.

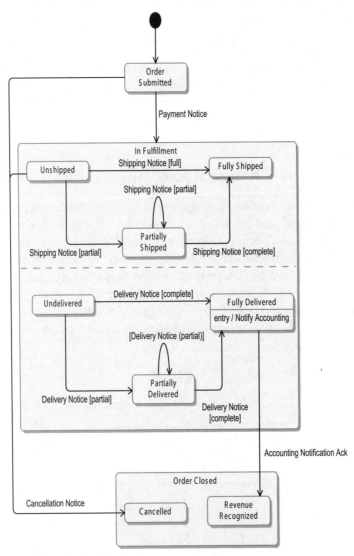

Figure 10-8: *Sales Order Life Cycle*

Continuous Query Change Recognition Pattern

Continuous queries (Chapter 7) can also be used to recognize change (Figure 10-9). Cached object changes or events directed to the cache agent enter the buffer if they meet the query selection criteria. Changes to the contents of the buffer trigger the reevaluation of the query. The query's callback function then examines the query results and determines whether a change notification is warranted.

When investigating fraudulent activity on accounts it is sometimes necessary to be notified in real time when there is activity on the account. The notification serves to prompt an investigator to immediately examine the activity and perhaps gather sufficient information to apprehend a suspect. Figure 10-10 shows how the activity alert could be generated by a continuous query set up to monitor the account. Note that there can be a number of these queries in operation at any given time, each monitoring a different account.

Handling Duplicate Events

When JMS is being used as the message transport, it is possible for a message to be delivered more than once even when a JMS queue is being used. The reason for this is that, by default, agents do not acknowledge message receipt until the work triggered by the message receipt is complete. This occurs at the end of the RTC cycle in an inference agent or when a checkpoint is taken in a process agent.

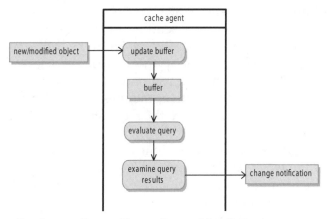

Figure 10-9: *Continuous Query Change Recognition Pattern*

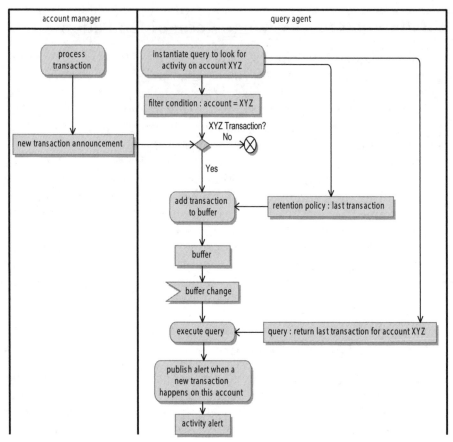

Figure 10-10: *Account Change Recognition*

Should an agent be shut down during the interval between the receipt of the message and the sending of the acknowledgment, the message becomes eligible for redelivery. From the JMS server perspective, this situation is signified by the loss of the socket connection between the JMS server and the component receiving the message. If another queue subscriber is active, the message will be immediately delivered to that subscriber. If not, the message will be delivered when the subscriber restarts.

The first question to ask when considering this scenario is, "Does it matter?" If the work being performed can be safely repeated (i.e., the activities are idempotent), then you don't have to do anything special to handle this situation. If the activities are not idempotent, then further consideration is required.

Recognize that there is no magic one-size-fits-all approach to solving this problem. What you need to do in the design depends to a great extent on the nature of the activity that cannot be repeated. However, TIBCO BusinessEvents provides you with the ability to recognize that the message has been redelivered. The incoming JMS message property `JMSRedelivered` indicates that the message has been redelivered. However, if you want to have access to this value in your logic, you need to define a Boolean `JMSRedelivered` property on the event.

The general strategy for handling message redelivery when there are non-idempotent activities is shown in Figure 10-11. When it appears as if a message has been redelivered, the first step is to investigate to determine how much of the normal processing was completed. With this information in hand, the required remaining activities can then be identified and performed.

Of course, this is just a sketch of the approach—the devil is in the details. Depending upon your design, you may implement this logic in preprocessor functions, rule conditions, or process orchestration exclusive gateways—or a combination of these. Some judgment is required as well. A lot of time and effort can be devoted to handling these situations. Be sure you clearly understand the negative consequences of repeating activities and adjust your design effort to be commensurate with the consequences.

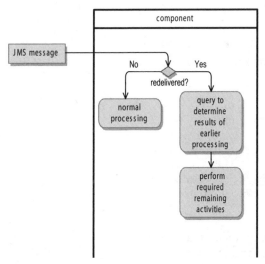

Figure 10-11: *Handling Message Redelivery for Non-idempotent Activities*

Enabling Run-Time Rule Changes

Some business requirements change faster than the normal IT project release cycle. Commonly these are the requirements for business rules that govern decisions, and the reason for the frequent change is to respond to changing market conditions. To make this possible, a mechanism is required that allows the business rule to be changed without requiring an IT change and subsequent deployment. Ideally, this type of change can be made by the business user directly, without requiring IT involvement.

The TIBCO BusinessEvents® Decision Manager extension provides two mechanisms that provide this capability, rule templates and decision tables, along with the Rules Management Server that administers these run-time modifications.

Rule Templates

A *rule template* is a variation of a rule that adds variables whose values can be changed at runtime (Listing 10-1). These variables are declared in the bindings section of the rule template. In this example, `tinyThreshold` and `giantThreshold` have been declared as variables. Both variables have initial values, but these values can be changed at runtime using the Rules Management Server. Thus the threshold values for identifying potential fraud with this pattern can be changed at runtime.

Listing 10-1: *ACEPSTRuleTemplate Example*

```
ruletemplate Rules.FraudRuleTemplate {
  attribute {priority = 5;forwardChain = true;}
  views{}
  bindings{
    double tinyThreshold = 5.0;
    double giantThreshold = 10000.0;
  }
  declare {
    Events.Transaction transactionA;
    Events.Transaction transactionB;
  }
  when {
    transactionB.transactionAmount <= tinyThreshold;
    transactionA.transactionAmount >= giantThreshold;
    transactionA.accountNumber == transactionB.accountNumber;
    transactionA.transactionDateTime > transactionB.
```

```
      transactionDateTime;
  }
  actionContext {
    System.debugOut("Fraud!");
  }
}
```

A rule template executes in exactly the same manner as an ordinary rule. When the variable values change, the changes are applied at the end of the RTC cycle. The mechanics of changing the values is discussed in the section on the Rules Management Server.

Decision Tables

Decision tables provide an implementation of the Decision as a Service Pattern from Figure 3-11. The implementation takes the form of a virtual rule function (Listing 10-2). The `scope` clause in the rule function defines the data structures that constitute the inputs and outputs of the decision service. Note that the body of the virtual rule function is empty—it is defined using a decision table.

Listing 10-2: *ACEPSTDecisionTable Virtual Rule Function*

```
virtual void rulefunction RuleFunctions.VirtualFraud {
  attribute {validity = ACTION;}
  scope {
    Events.Transaction transactionA;
    Events.Transaction transactionB;
    Concepts.FraudRuleResult fraudruleresult;
  }
  body {

  }
}
```

The body of a virtual rule function is specified using a decision table (Figure 10-12). The columns of the table identify the input data elements (Condition Area) and output data elements (Action Area) from the rule's scope. The entries in the Condition Area represent the rule's conditions. For example, the first column is headed `transactionA. transactionAmount`, and the entry in the first (and only) row is `>=10000`; that is, the first condition for the row is that transaction A's amount is greater than or equal to 10000.

The Action Area specifies the formula for computing each output value should all the conditions in the row evaluate to `true`. In the

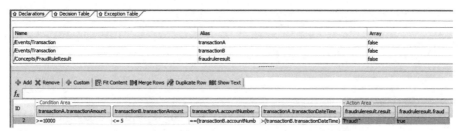

Figure 10-12: *ACEPSTDecisionTable Virtual Rule Function Implementation*

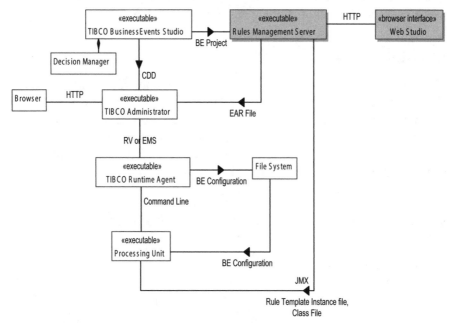

Figure 10-13: *Rules Management Server (RMS) Administrative Configuration*

example, the `result` field receives the string value "`Fraud!`" and the fraud `boolean` is set to `true`.

Rule Management Server (RMS)

Rule templates and decision tables set the stage for run-time changes, but the actual run-time modification is achieved using the Rules Management Server (RMS). The life cycle of a solution is a bit different when RMS is used (Figure 10-13). RMS projects are placed in a specially configured directory (details are in the *Developer's Guide*), and the EAR file is actually generated by the Rules Management Server. This makes the project RMS-aware and sets the stage for run-time modification of rule templates and decision tables.

Once the EAR file has been generated, deployment proceeds normally. At runtime, the Web Studio browser interface to the Rules Management Server can be used to modify the variables of a rule template or replace a decision table. For ease of editing by nontechnical personnel, decision tables can be exported to Excel spreadsheets, modified, imported, and deployed. RMS supports an approval process for deployment.

Sequential and Conditional Action Performance

Many solutions require that a number of actions either be performed sequentially or conditionally. There are a number of ways in which this can be accomplished in TIBCO BusinessEvents. These include

- Orchestration implemented in the action section of a single rule
- Having a separate rule for each action
- Orchestration implemented in an explicit orchestration component

Orchestration Implemented in the Action Section of a Single Rule

This is a straightforward approach, with the action section of the rule implementing the necessary logic. Locking can be implemented as required, and the presence of all the logic in a single block of code makes it easy to understand the flow.

While this approach is straightforward, it is not capable of performing asynchronous interactions: There is no mechanism for receiving an asynchronous response in the action part of a rule. Asynchronous responses would have to be treated as independent events and thus cannot be handled in the action section of the rule sending the request.

From an efficiency perspective, placing the logic in the action part of a rule is often the most efficient implementation. However, it does tie up the thread running the RTC.

Having a Separate Rule for Each Action

An alternative to a block of logic with an if-then-else structure is to use a series of independent rules, one for each action. Each rule specifies the conditions for executing its associated action.

If the rules are truly independent, this approach can simplify the maintenance of the individual action invocations and their associated logic. But there are drawbacks as well.

One drawback is that because the logic is now distributed across a number of rules, it is more difficult to understand the overall behavior. From a performance perspective, distributing the logic in this manner is demonstrably less efficient in terms of overhead than executing all the logic in a single rule action, particularly if there are common conditions across multiple rules.

But the biggest drawback may be the assumption that the logic for each of the actions is truly independent. If you are trying to implement if-then-else logic, there is a sequencing dependency: The "else" clause is only executed when the "if" clause is not executed. This requires some sequential coordination, and some additional design work, to achieve this sequencing.

Sequencing the Execution of Rules

There are two mechanisms for managing the sequential execution of rules in TIBCO BusinessEvents: priority and rank. Rule priority is established at design time, while rule rank is computed dynamically at runtime when the rule is placed in the rule agenda (see Chapter 5). When the rule agenda is sorted, rules are sorted by priority first, and then by rank within priority.

The challenge with priority and rank is one of clarity. Understanding the overall prioritization and ranking scheme can be complex, particularly when there are multiple situations requiring sequencing. This scheme must be clearly understood by anyone creating rules that are involved in the sequencing. And since producing the proper sequencing requires that this scheme be properly applied in every rule, testing whether the desired sequencing has actually been achieved can be even more complex.

For these reasons, schemes involving priority and rank should be used sparingly. Two common applications are executing clean-up logic and detecting exceptions. In both cases, these are functions that you want to perform after all of the normal processing has been completed. Since, by default, rules run at priority 5, you might want to set up your clean-up logic rules to run at priority 9, and your exception detection logic to run at priority 10 (assuming it does not need to be part of the mainstream work). Of course, these prioritization policies must be clearly understood by everyone involved in order for them to work!

Orchestration Implemented in an Explicit Orchestration Component

Orchestration components are designed to coordinate the execution of multiple activities and thus are well-suited for the task. TIBCO BusinessEvents® Process Orchestration, TIBCO ActiveMatrix BusinessWorks™, and TIBCO ActiveMatrix® BPM are all viable candidates for this role. Broadly speaking, TIBCO BusinessEvents Process Orchestration fits when rule-driven logic plays a significant role, ActiveMatrix BusinessWorks fits when the orchestration involves a lot of integration, and ActiveMatrix BPM when there is a workforce involved.

Employing an explicit orchestration component requires coordination between the TIBCO BusinessEvents agent initiating the work and the orchestration component. Initiating the orchestration work simply involves sending a request (an event) to the orchestration component. However, you need to think about the coordination pattern that will be used and how your choice impacts the solution's ability to detect breakdowns in the process. The basic choices are

- Fire and Forget: Just send the request; no breakdown detection possible
- Request Reply (synchronous or asynchronous): Reply confirms successful completion of coordinated work; requires timeout to detect breakdown
- Delegation with Confirmation: Immediate reply indicates responsibility has been transferred; eventual asynchronous confirmation indicates successful completion of coordinated work; requires timeout to detect breakdown

A more detailed description of these coordination patterns can be found in *TIBCO™ Architecture Fundamentals*.[1]

The Asynchronous Request-Reply and Delegation with Confirmation patterns each require some logic to track the response and determine whether the response was delivered within the expected time frame. This is an ideal application for a state machine (Figure 10-14). When this machine is started, it sends the Request event and enters the Request Sent state, which starts the timer. It remains in that state until one of two things happens: the Response event is received or a

---

1. Paul C. Brown, *TIBCO® Architecture Fundamentals*, Boston: Addison-Wesley (2011).

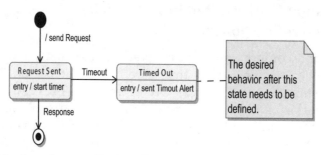

Figure 10-14: *Asynchronous Request-Response State Machine*

`Timeout` occurs. Receiving the `Response` event completes the execution of the state machine. If a `Timeout` occurs, a `Timeout Alert` is sent, but the subsequent behavior still needs to be added to this state machine. It is important to explore recovery behaviors for critical processes while your design is still in its formative stages; these behaviors can be difficult to retrofit into a design.

Logging and Exception Reporting

Virtually every solution you define will require some form of logging and exception reporting. Each processing unit has a log file configuration defined in the CDD file for the cluster. The choice of logging levels determines the amount of information logged. The CDD file defines the default level, but the logging level can be changed at runtime using the Hawk AMI interface or the BEMM interface.

The Data Grid underlying the cache agent is an implementation of TIBCO ActiveSpaces®. Its log settings are set via the CDD properties (see the *Developer's Guide* for details).

For inference, query, and process agents, additional reporting can be managed via rule functions. Here, logic can be added to either generate events or make log file entries. However, be sure to consider the performance implications—disk activity can slow down a design!

Naming Guidelines

In an event-driven system, there is a tendency to name rules and rule functions in a way that identifies the event or situation that triggers their execution. Unfortunately, in terms of understanding a design, this type of naming is not particularly useful: You end up having to look at each rule and rule function in order to understand what it does. This leads to the following best practice recommendations:

- The name of a rule should indicate the type of situation being recognized by the conditions of the rule.

- The name of the rule function should indicate the intended use of the rule function. In particular, rule functions intended to be used as preprocessor or start-up functions should be labeled as such.

- The name of the event should identify the situation whose existence is being announced by the event.

Summary

Changes in situations can be recognized in many ways. Trivially, an event may itself announce the change. In more complex situations, you may need to compare the event's representation of current status against reference data to determine whether a change has occurred.

If the reference data is not static, the event that you are comparing against the reference data may also result in a reference-data update. Here, the coordination of the comparison and the reference data update must be considered, as well as the system-of-record for the reference data.

When the situation being monitored is complex, the use of a state machine or continuous query may be warranted.

Abrupt shutdowns when JMS messaging is being used for input events can lead to the duplicate delivery of messages. Duplicates can be detected by adding a `JMSRedelivered` property to the incoming event. This property can then be used to trigger additional logic to determine how much prior work had been completed and adjust activity performance accordingly.

Some situations require changing business logic at runtime. TIBCO BusinessEvents provides two mechanisms that provide this capability: rule templates that allow constant values in rules to be altered and decision tables that allow the mapping of input data to results to be modified at runtime.

Some situations require multiple activities to be performed. There are several approaches that can be used to coordinate these activities: Execute all the activities in the action part of a rule; use a separate rule for each action, possibly using priority and rank to control the sequence of execution; or use an external orchestration component. In the latter case, if the process is critical, a state machine can be used to manage the dialog with the coordination component and detect breakdowns.

TIBCO BusinessEvents has built-in logging that can be configured in the CDD file. Additional logging and exception reporting can be added via rule functions in inference, query, and process agents.

Naming best practices will make your design easier to understand. The name of the rule should indicate the condition recognized by the rule. The name of a function should indicate its intended role in the solution. The name of an event should identify the situation whose existence is being announced by the event.

Chapter 11

Event Pattern Recognition

Objectives

The TIBCO BusinessEvents® Event Stream Processing extension includes features for recognizing patterns of events. This chapter explores these capabilities. After reading this chapter, you will be able to describe how these patterns are defined and how the pattern recognition is deployed. You will also be able to describe how patterns can be used for component liveness monitoring.

The Need for Event Pattern Recognition

Some patterns of events are awkward to recognize using rules. Consider the following example:

- Three red balls
- Followed by two blue balls
- Followed by one yellow ball

You could, of course, craft a state machine to recognize this pattern (Figure 11-1). The problem with this approach is that as the pattern gets

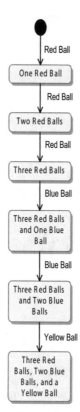

Figure 11-1: *State Machine Pattern Recognizer*

more complex, it becomes increasingly difficult and tedious to craft the state machine—and verify that the pattern that it recognizes is the pattern you are trying to recognize.

Another dimension of complexity is the introduction of time constraints. Consider this variation:

- Three red balls within five minutes
- Followed by two blue balls within 30 seconds
- Followed by a yellow ball within an hour

Again, you could craft a state machine to recognize this pattern (Figure 11-2), but the increasing complexity of doing so is beginning to become apparent.

From a recognition perspective, the state machine is the right tool to use. The problem lies in the crafting of the machine. The traditional computer science answer to this problem is to define a pattern language, an accompanying compiler that automatically generates the

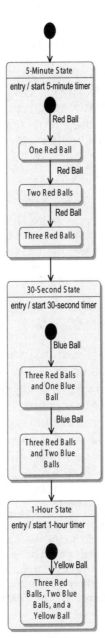

Figure 11-2: *State Machine Pattern Recognizer with Timeouts*

state machine, and a run-time environment in which the state machine can be applied to recognize the patterns. The TIBCO BusinessEvents Event Stream Processing extension provides these capabilities for recognizing patterns of events.

Event Stream Processing Pattern Language

Listing 11-1 shows the ball example expressed in the pattern language provided by the TIBCO BusinessEvents Event Stream Processing extension. The `using` clause identifies the types of events involved in the pattern and the aliases for those events used in the pattern definition. The actual pattern description begins with the `starts` keyword.

Listing 11-1: *Ball Pattern Example*

```
define pattern Ball Pattern
    using /Events/Trigger as trigger
        and /Events/RedBall as redBall
        and /Events/BlueBall as blueBall
        and /Events/YellowBall as yellowBall
    starts with trigger
        then within 5 minutes (redBall then redBall then
            redBall)
        then within 30 seconds (blueBall then blueBall)
        then within 1 hour yellowBall;
```

The pattern language is described in great detail in the *Pattern Matcher's Developer's Guide* that comes with the extension, so it will not be explored further here except to point out one additional feature. Listing 11-2 shows a pattern that can be used to recognize the fraud pattern that is being used in many of the examples. This example contains a `with` clause. The first term in the clause identifies a property whose value must match an identified property of each of the other events. The clause effectively defines a join.

Listing 11-2: *ACEPSTPattern Example*

```
define pattern ACEPSTPattern
    using /Events/TinyTransaction as tinyTransaction
        and /Events/GiantTransaction as giantTransaction
    with tinyTransaction.accountNumber
        and giantTransaction.accountNumber
    starts with tinyTransaction then within 1 hour
        giantTransaction;
```

Using a Pattern

Putting a pattern to use involves more than the pattern definition (Figure 11-3). The process of defining the pattern creates a class that is the named pattern. To put the pattern to use, instances of the pattern

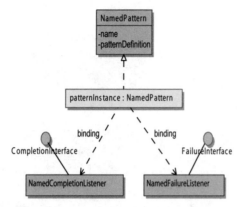

Figure 11-3: *Pattern Elements*

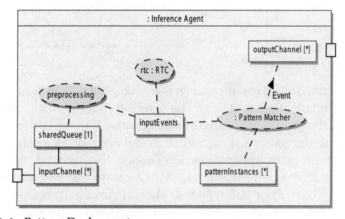

Figure 11-4: *Pattern Deployment*

(instances of the class) are created. Each instance requires two callback functions, one to be called when the pattern is recognized and the other to be called when the pattern fails. These callback functions have fixed signatures. Once the instance has been created, values can be assigned to any variables in the pattern definition.

Patterns are deployed in inference agents (Figure 11-4). The processing of patterns is handled by a pool of threads dedicated to the pattern matcher. Events are sent to the pattern matcher either by preprocessor functions or rule actions using the `Pattern.IO.toPattern()` function. The pattern callback functions can create events and send them to channels, but it cannot interact with concepts. The size of the pattern matcher thread pool can be set with the `Pattern.Manager.Advanced.setPoolSize()` function.

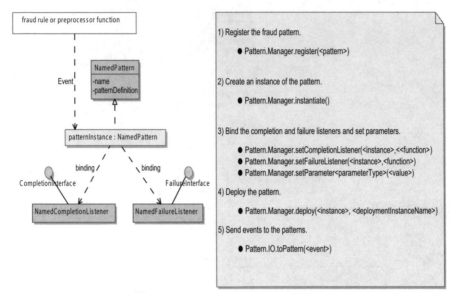

Figure 11-5: *Pattern Life Cycle*

The actual deployment process is managed by code running in the inference agent (Figure 11-5). The process begins with the call to `Pattern.Manager.register(<pattern>)` that creates the class representing the pattern. Typically, this call is made in a start-up function, but it can be made anywhere a catalog function can be invoked. An instance of the pattern is made with a call to `Pattern.Manager.instantiate()`. For patterns that should run continuously, this call is made in the start-up function. For patterns that only run under certain circumstances, this call is made either in a preprocessor function in response to an event that announces that these circumstances exist or in the action part of a rule that recognizes these circumstances. Wherever the instantiation is done, the completion listener and failure listener must be set along with the values of any parameters. Once these actions are complete, the pattern can be deployed.

Liveness Monitoring

One application of patterns is liveness monitoring. From time to time it may be necessary to determine whether a particular component is operational. One approach to making this determination is to have the component send a periodic heartbeat and use pattern recognition to

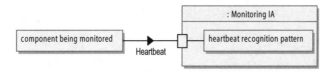

Figure 11-6: *Heartbeat Recognition*

determine whether the component is still operational (Figure 11-6). For example, the component might send a heartbeat event once every three seconds. The pattern might be that there should be at least one heartbeat in a ten-second sliding window of time. The absence of heartbeats for ten seconds would then constitute a failure of the pattern.

Summary

Complex patterns can be difficult to recognize using rules and hand-crafted state machines. For this reason the TIBCO BusinessEvents Event Stream Processor extensions provide a pattern recognition language that makes it easy to define patterns of interest. This language is used to automatically create state machines that recognize the specified patterns.

Patterns are deployed in inference agents. Events must be explicitly sent to the pattern matcher either by the preprocessor or the action part of a rule. When a match is made, the completion listener callback function is invoked; and if the pattern fails to match, the failure listener callback function is invoked.

The life cycle of a pattern is managed by code running in the inference agent. This code defines the pattern, creates instances, sets the callback functions and variable values, and deploys the pattern. The code performing these functions can be located in start-up functions, preprocessor functions, or the action part of a rule.

Patterns can be used for component liveness monitoring. If a component is expected to send a heartbeat periodically, a pattern can be used to recognize the absence of the heartbeats and conclude that the component is no longer operational.

Chapter 12

Integration

Objectives

The components that provide complex-event processing capabilities cannot live in isolation. Most of the events to which they react originate in other systems, and many of the actions they take are implemented by other systems. Integration with these systems is key.

Integration is a broad topic, much of which is beyond the scope of this book. The basics of integration and services are covered in *TIBCO*™ *Architecture Fundamentals*[1]; more advanced related topics are covered in *Architecting Composite Applications and Services with TIBCO*™.[2] These books describe some TIBCO™ products commonly used in conjunction with TIBCO BusinessEvents®: TIBCO ActiveMatrix BusinessWorks™, TIBCO ActiveMatrix® Adapter for Database, TIBCO ActiveMatrix® Adapter for Files, and TIBCO Enterprise Message Service™, among others. They also cover SOA concepts and design patterns involving these products.

1. Paul C. Brown, *TIBCO® Architecture Fundamentals*, Boston: Addison-Wesley (2011).

2. Paul C. Brown, *Architecting Composite Applications and Services with TIBCO®*, Boston: Addison-Wesley (2012).

TIBCO BusinessEvents can, of course, interact via its channels with any component using a supported transport. There are also additional integration capabilities in the product. This chapter explores these additional integration capabilities. After reading this chapter you will be able to describe how TIBCO BusinessEvents can interact with:

- TIBCO ActiveMatrix BusinessWorks™
- Web services
- Databases

Interacting with TIBCO ActiveMatrix BusinessWorks™

TIBCO ActiveMatrix BusinessWorks™ has a plugin to simplify interactions with TIBCO BusinessEvents®. The use of the plugin enables ActiveMatrix BusinessWorks to define RuleServiceProvider Configurations. Each of these configurations contains pointers to the EAR and CDD files from a TIBCO BusinessEvents project with which you want to interact. The configuration also identifies a processing unit that is defined in the CDD file. When the ActiveMatrix BusinessWorks engine runs, it will run an instance of this processing unit in the same JVM as the ActiveMatrix BusinessWorks engine.[3]

The plugin provides four activities that can be employed in ActiveMatrix BusinessWorks processes: (1) Send Event, (2) Receive Event, (3) Wait for Event, and (4) Invoke RuleFunction.

TIBCO ActiveMatrix Business Works™ Send Event

The Send Event activity enables ActiveMatrix BusinessWorks to send an event to a specific destination in a processing unit (Figure 12-1). The configuration of this activity shows the event data structure so that values can be readily mapped to the event properties. Executing the activity sends the event to the specified destination.

---

3. A similar integration, in which an instance of TIBCO ActiveMatrix BusinessWorks executed in the same JVM as a processing unit, has been deprecated as of the 5.x release of TIBCO BusinessEvents.

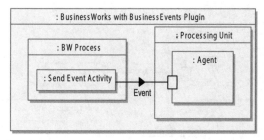

Figure 12-1: *TIBCO ActiveMatrix Business Works™ Sending an Event*

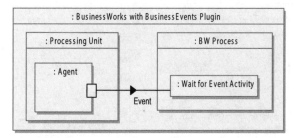

Figure 12-2: *TIBCO ActiveMatrix BusinessWorks™ Waiting for an Event*

TIBCO ActiveMatrix BusinessWorks™ Wait for Event

The Wait for Event activity is a blocking activity in an ActiveMatrix BusinessWorks process (Figure 12-2). When the process executes the activity, it waits for TIBCO BusinessEvents to send the event. The properties of the event are available to the ActiveMatrix BusinessWorks process.

The Wait for Event activity can be used in conjunction with the Send Event activity to implement a synchronous request-reply interaction between ActiveMatrix BusinessWorks and TIBCO BusinessEvents.

TIBCO ActiveMatrix Business Works™ Receive Event

The TIBCO ActiveMatrix Receive Event activity is an ActiveMatrix BusinessWorks process starter (Figure 12-3). When TIBCO BusinessEvents sends an event of the indicated type, the ActiveMatrix BusinessWorks process starter receives the event and creates an instance of the process that uses that event as its process starter. The properties of the event are available for use in the process.

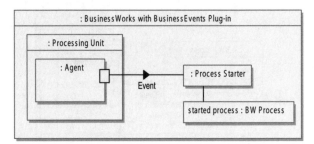

Figure 12-3: *TIBCO ActiveMatrix BusinessWorks™ Receiving an Event*

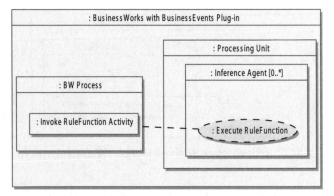

Figure 12-4: *Invoking a RuleFunction*

The Receive Event activity can be used in conjunction with the Send Event activity to implement an asynchronous request-reply interaction between TIBCO BusinessEvents and ActiveMatrix BusinessWorks.

Invoke RuleFunction

The fourth activity executes a rule function in an agent of the embedded processing unit (Figure 12-4). The function executes in a thread from a pool dedicated to these requests. By default, this thread acquires a lock on the RTC. It will not run until the current RTC cycle completes, and it will keep other RTC cycles from executing until the function execution is complete.

TIBCO BusinessEvents® as a Service Provider

TIBCO BusinessEvents can readily play the role of a service provider (Figure 12-5). Any of the channel types (see Chapter 5) can be used for transport, ranging from SOAP over HTTP or JMS to raw TCP

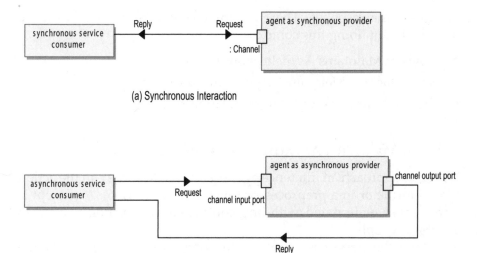

(a) Synchronous Interaction

(b) Asynchronous Interaction

Figure 12-5: *TIBCO BusinessEvents® as a Service Provider*

socket connections. Commonly an inference agent is used as the service provider, but process agents and even query agents can play this role as well.

In most situations, when the agent is playing the role of a service provider, the receipt of the request is the triggering event for all of the processing required to produce the result. After receipt of the request, processing continues until the result is produced.

In some situations, when the agent plays the role of an asynchronous provider, the receipt of the request does not trigger all of the work: Some remainder of the work is performed in response to another event. In some situations this event is directly related to the request—a timer expiring or an asynchronous response from some back-end system. In other situations, the other event may be an update to a cached concept whose change triggers the generation of the response (see Reference-Data Change Coordination pattern in Chapter 10).

TIBCO BusinessEvents® as an Asynchronous Service Consumer

Consuming services with an asynchronous interaction is fairly straightforward with TIBCO BusinessEvents. However, asynchronous interactions generally require the retention of contextual information required to process the response. There are three design patterns that can be used for maintaining this context:

- Concept Maintains Asynchronous Context
- State Machine Maintains Asynchronous Context
- Process Maintains Asynchronous Context

Concept Maintains Asynchronous Context

With this approach an inference agent sends the `Request` in the action part of a rule or in a preprocessor function (Figure 12-6). A concept is also created or updated with any contextual information needed to process the reply.

When the `Reply` is returned, the preprocessor function for the reply event retrieves the concept from the cache (assuming cache-only mode was used). To make retrieval possible, the identifier for the concept (typically the `extID`) must be included in the request and returned in the reply. The service provider must also be designed to return the identifier from the request in the reply. If JMS is used for the transport and the `extID` of the concept is used as the `JMSCorrelationID` of the request, the JMS specification requires that the service provider pass this same value back as the `JMSCorrelationID` of the reply. The reply is then processed either in the preprocessor function or in rules triggered by the arrival of the reply event.

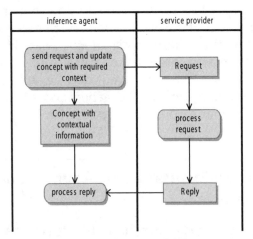

Figure 12-6: *Concept Maintains Asynchronous Context*

In sending the `Request`, if the concept that will hold the context already exists, the `Request` must be sent in the action part of the rule since a preprocessor function cannot modify an existing concept—it can only create a new concept.

State Machine Maintains Asynchronous State

The TIBCO BusinessEvents® Data Modeling extension adds state machine capabilities to concepts. This makes possible a pattern that uses a state machine to maintain the asynchronous state and also to manage the entire interaction. A sketch of such a state machine is shown in Figure 12-7.

Recall that a state machine is owned by a concept (Chapter 5). When the state machine starts, the `Request` it sends contains as a data element the `extID` of the concept owning the state machine. This `extID` is expected to be returned in the `Reply` and will be used to correlate the reply with this particular state machine instance. The state machine then enters a state where it is waiting for a reply. When a reply arrives with a matching `extID`, the machine makes another transition.

As for actions to be taken when the reply is received, there are two possible approaches. One is that the actions can be part of the state machine structure, executed when state transitions are taken or when states are entered or exited. The other approach is to place actions in the action part of a rule that is triggered when a change occurs to the state machine. From a rule perspective, this is a change to the concept that owns the state machine.

One advantage of this approach is that the state machine has timer infrastructure that can be used to recognize that a reply has not been received within a designated period of time.

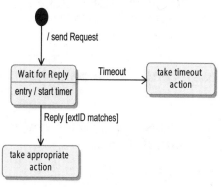

Figure 12-7: *State Machine Maintains Asynchronous State*

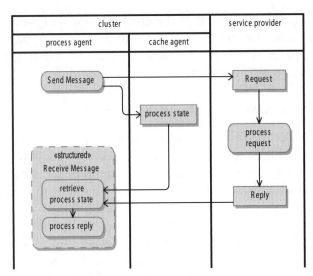

Figure 12-8: *Process Maintains Asynchronous State*

Process Maintains Asynchronous State

The TIBCO BusinessEvents® Process Orchestration extension provides process agents that are well-suited to asynchronous service interactions (Figure 12-8). The `SendMessage` activity is used to send the `Request`. When the message is sent, the process agent automatically checkpoints the process to the cache. The `Request` must contain the `extID` of the process as one of its data elements, and the service provider must include it as part of the `Reply`.

The `ReceiveMessage` activity is used to receive the `Reply`. When the `Reply` is received, the process agent retrieves the state of the process from the cache using the `extID`. It then executes the activity.

When you use process orchestration, you must remember that the process agent cannot be deployed in the same cluster as inference agents.

TIBCO BusinessEvents® as a Synchronous Service Consumer

There are three mechanisms available for synchronous service consumption in TIBCO BusinessEvents:

1. HTTP Send Request Invocation
2. Process Orchestration Web Service Invocation
3. Custom Function Invocation

HTTP Send Request Invocation

This pattern uses the catalog HTTP function `sendRequest()`. It can be used for both conventional HTTP request-reply interactions and for SOAP interactions (Figure 12-9). Care should be exercised when using this pattern, as the thread making the call is tied up while waiting for the reply. When there are many threads available, such as when executing a preprocessor function, the blocked thread may be only a condition to be considered when deciding the size of the thread pool. However, when the function is executed in the action part of a rule and the RTC is configured to be single threaded, all RTC processing will be blocked until the request completes.

TIBCO BusinessEvents® Process Orchestration Web Service Invocation

The TIBCO BusinessEvents Process Orchestration extension includes a Web Service task, which is used for synchronous service invocations (Figure 12-10). Recall that all tasks are executed by a pool of threads in

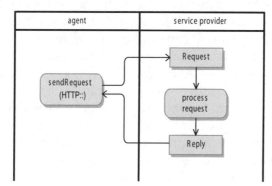

Figure 12-9: *HTTP Send Request Invocation*

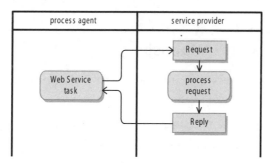

Figure 12-10: *TIBCO BusinessEvents® Process Orchestration Web Service Invocation*

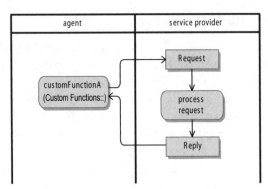

Figure 12-11: *Custom Function Invocation Pattern*

the process agent (Chapter 8). From a performance perspective, increasing the number of threads in this pool can compensate for the fact that the thread is blocked during the call.

Custom Function Invocation

TIBCO BusinessEvents provides the ability to define custom functions. These functions are written in Java and can employ Java libraries, thus making all of the Java I/O capabilities available. Thus you can implement a custom function that makes a synchronous call to a service provider (Figure 12-11). As with the HTTP Send Request Invocation pattern, this pattern should be used with care: The thread executing the function will be tied up waiting for the service provider to respond. If the thread is from a pool of threads operating concurrently (e.g., in a preprocessor function), then increasing the number of threads can compensate for this. On the other hand, if the function is being executed in the action part of a rule and RTC is configured single threaded, all RTC processing will be blocked while this function executes.

Interacting with Databases

TIBCO BusinessEvents can interact with a database using three patterns. These include

1. Database Interaction Using Database Concepts
2. Database Interaction Using TIBCO ActiveMatrix® Adapter for Database
3. Database Interaction Using TIBCO ActiveMatrix BusinessWorks™

Database Interaction Using Database Concepts

The TIBCO BusinessEvents Data Modeling extension provides the ability to automatically define concepts that correspond to database tables. Rows in the database table correspond to instances of the database concept. The extension also provides a collection of related RDBMS catalog functions.

Database Concepts and Memory Management

Database concepts operate differently than ordinary concepts. The default memory management mode for database concepts is Memory Only—concepts reside only in the inference agent. Furthermore, a database concept that is created or updated as a result of an RDBMS query is not automatically placed in working memory. It must be explicitly asserted using the `Database.assertDBInstance()` catalog function.

By exception, database concepts can be configured as Cache Only or Cache + Memory. However, backing store is never an option for a database concept. Even if the cluster is configured for backing store, these settings will be ignored for database concepts.

Database Query

Database queries run against the database and return database concepts as results (Figure 12-12). These concepts are then available for subsequent processing in the agent. There are a number of RDBMS functions available for queries. If large result sets are expected, there are catalog functions for working with database cursors and walking through result sets.

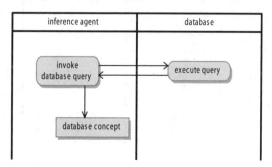

Figure 12-12: *Database Query*

Database Update and Delete

While an inference agent can make changes to a database concept, those changes are not automatically saved in the database. An explicit call to the RDBMS catalog function `Database.update()` is required (Figure 12-13).

Conversely, changes in the database itself are not automatically reflected in the database concept, nor is there any automatic mechanism for knowing that the database has changed (see the section on using TIBCO ActiveMatrix® Adapter for Database). In order to get updated database information into database concepts, another query is required.

A database deletion can be performed with a call to the RDBMS function `Database.delete()`. Deletions in the database itself are not automatically reflected in the database concept. Recognizing a database deletion requires removing the database concept from memory and then repeating the query.

Database Interaction Using TIBCO ActiveMatrix® Adapter for Database

The TIBCO ActiveMatrix® Adapter for Database can also be used for database interactions (Figure 12-14). The adapter communicates with the target database using the JDBC or ODBC protocols.

There are three interaction patterns possible with the adapter:

1. Inference Agent Publication
2. Inference Agent Request-Reply
3. Inference Agent Subscription

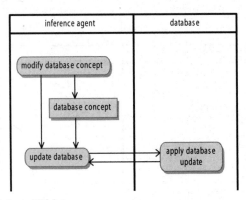

Figure 12-13: *Database Update*

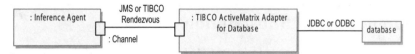

Figure 12-14: *Database Adapter Configuration*

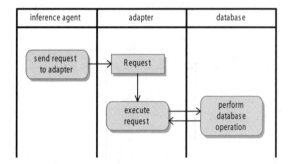

Figure 12-15: *Inference Agent Publication*

Inference Agent Publication

In this pattern, the inference agent publishes a request to the adapter (Figure 12-15). The adapter, in turn, performs the requested database operation. This is an in-only operation: No reply is generated for the request. The adapter provides several SQL operations that can be invoked in this manner:

- Insert
- Update
- Delete
- Insert/Update (update if the row exists, otherwise insert)

Inference Agent Request-Reply

The adapter provides the capability of executing SQL statements and stored procedures via a request-reply interaction (Figure 12-16). In employing this capability, the inference agent would use one of the asynchronous consumer patterns described earlier in this chapter.

Inference Agent Subscription

This pattern is used to inform the inference agent of changes to the database (Figure 12-17). During adapter configuration to publish changes from a database table, a trigger is placed in the database. When a database change occurs, a snapshot of the affected database record is

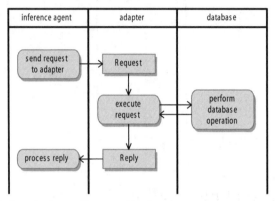

Figure 12-16: *Inference Agent Request-Reply*

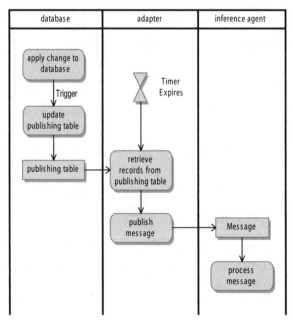

Figure 12-17: *Inference Agent Subscription*

placed in a publishing table. The adapter periodically checks to see whether there are any entries in the publishing table and, if there are, publishes a message for each entry. If the inference agent is a subscriber to these messages, it will receive the notifications of database change and can take whatever actions are appropriate for the application.

Database Interaction Using TIBCO ActiveMatrix BusinessWorks™

Using TIBCO ActiveMatrix BusinessWorks to perform the database interactions requires using a combination of two or three design patterns described earlier:

- TIBCO BusinessEvents as an Asynchronous Service Consumer
- ActiveMatrix BusinessWorks Receive Event
- ActiveMatrix BusinessWorks Send Event

Using the Asynchronous Service Consumer pattern, TIBCO BusinessEvents sends the request to ActiveMatrix BusinessWorks, which uses the ActiveMatrix BusinessWorks Receive Event pattern to start a process that will perform the database update(s) and perhaps other operations as well. Optionally, the process can employ the ActiveMatrix BusinessWorks Send Event pattern to report results back to TIBCO BusinessEvents.

The advantage of this pattern is that the full integration capabilities of ActiveMatrix BusinessWorks can be brought to bear. The database update can be performed as part of an XA transaction, and it can be coordinated with other activities as well.

Summary

TIBCO BusinessEvents processing units can be deployed in TIBCO ActiveMatrix BusinessWorks engines. A palette of ActiveMatrix BusinessWorks activities enables ActiveMatrix BusinessWorks to interact with TIBCO BusinessEvents channels. ActiveMatrix BusinessWorks can use these activities to send events, wait for events, and invoke TIBCO BusinessEvents rule functions. There is also a process starter activity that can be used to define a process that can be started by TIBCO BusinessEvents sending a message.

TIBCO BusinessEvents can play the role of a service provider using a channel as the service interface. It can also play the role of a service consumer, with both asynchronous and synchronous interactions. There are a number of design patterns that can be used for this purpose. When TIBCO BusinessEvents is a synchronous service consumer, careful consideration has to be given as to where the operation is performed, because it will tie up the execution thread while waiting for the operation to complete.

There are several options for TIBCO BusinessEvents to interact with databases. The TIBCO BusinessEvents Data Modeling extension provides the automatic definition of concepts that correspond to database tables and a set of RDBMS catalog functions for interacting with the database. Database concepts behave differently than ordinary concepts. By default, they are managed Memory Only, and they do not appear in working memory unless explicitly asserted. Database concepts must be explicitly loaded from the database, and changes to database concepts must be explicitly applied to the database.

The TIBCO ActiveMatrix Adapter for Database can also be used for database interactions, with a messaging channel (JMS or TIBCO Rendezvous®) as the interface to the adapter. There are three interaction patterns that can be used. The use of the adapter makes it possible to inform TIBCO BusinessEvents of changes to the database.

Interactions with a database can also be delegated to ActiveMatrix BusinessWorks. This provides the ability to execute XA transactions and coordinate the database update with other activities.

Chapter 13

Solution Modularization Patterns

Objectives

While rule-based approaches are powerful and flexible, without some discipline in organizing your rule-based solution you are liable to end up with a spaghetti-code nightmare. This chapter covers a number of patterns you can use to organize your solution and avoid this problem. After reading this chapter you will be able to

- Explain two major principles that can be used for partitioning (modularizing) a solution
- Explain the design patterns that arise from partitioning
- Explain the advantages and disadvantages of partitioning
- Describe the rules of thumb for partitioning

Partitioning Situation Recognition from Action

The characteristic pattern of an event-driven process (Figure 2-11) is also a best practice for partitioning logic in a design (Figure 13-1). In this pattern, the logic of recognizing that a particular situation exists is separated from the logic of what to do now that the situation has been recognized. The recognition that the situation exists is announced by sending an event, and the subsequent action is triggered by the arrival of that event.

When situation recognition and the execution of the action both involve complex logic, mixing the logic together makes it difficult to clearly understand the logic behind either. Partitioning the two not only adds clarity but simplifies logic maintenance as well. It also makes it trivially easy to add additional actions in response to the event.

Partitioning in this manner does not necessarily require that the two roles are being played by different agents. The situation announcement event could be locally asserted by an inference agent, triggering separate rules in the same agent that manages the required action (Figure 13-2). In this case, the partitioning primarily provides a modularization of the rules for ease of understanding and maintenance.

A second alternative is to deploy the rules to two agents running in the same processing unit using a local channel for communications (Figure 13-3). Since each agent has its own working memory, the management of working memory can be simpler, provided different concepts are needed for recognition and action. Since each agent has its

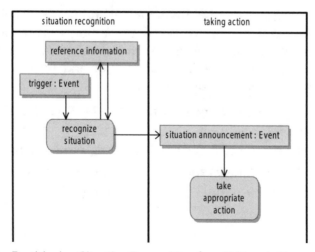

Figure 13-1: *Partitioning Situation Recognition from Taking Action*

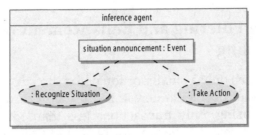

Figure 13-2: *Partitioning with Single Agent Deployment*

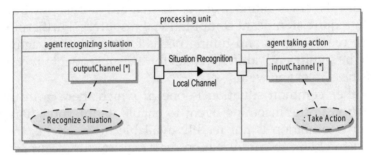

Figure 13-3: *Partitioning with Single Processing Unit Deployment*

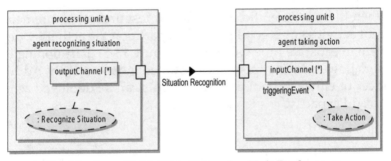

Figure 13-4: *Partitioning with Multiple Processing Unit Deployment*

own RTC cycle, the operation of one will not have an adverse impact on the other provided the processing unit as a whole has sufficient resources.

A third alternative is to deploy the two agents in different processing units (Figure 13-4). Although this incurs the overhead of inter-process communication, the two roles can now be tuned and scaled independently. Indeed, multiple instances of either or both processing units can be deployed as needed to handle the load.

Partitioning Filtering and Enhancement from Rule Processing

In many situations only a small portion of the directly observable technical events are of business interest. In the credit card fraud example we have been using, only transactions less than $5 or greater than $10,000 are of interest. The vast majority of credit card transactions are likely to lie between these two thresholds.

In situations like this, the task of filtering the raw technical events to identify the small number of events that are of business interest is likely to require significant computational resources. Furthermore, the resource requirements and tuning needs for the filtering activity are liable to be significantly different than for the subsequent processing of the business-relevant events.

Another common situation is one in which there is insufficient information in the incoming event to enable its interpretation. If the required information is not readily available in the cache, the work required to obtain this information may require significant computational resources. The resource and tuning requirements for this activity are likely to be significantly different than those for the subsequent processing of the event.

When there are significantly different resourcing requirements for different activities, it is good practice to partition the activities, deploying them in separate processing units (Figure 13-5). Partitioning in this manner allows each component to be tuned independently. Additional instances of either or both processing units can be deployed as necessary to add capacity.

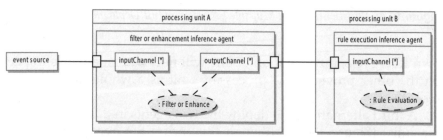

Figure 13-5: *Partitioning Filtering and Enhancement from Rule Processing*

When this pattern is employed, the filtering and enrichment inference agent typically performs the filtering and/or enrichment in preprocessor functions and sends the resulting event directly to the output channel. This allows the agent to employ the shared thread pool for these activities. Very often there are no rules deployed to this agent.

There is an additional consideration when using this pattern for enrichment: how the additional information is going to be conveyed to the rule execution inference agent. The best practice in this situation is to define a new type of event that contains both the information from the technical event and the additional information required for the processing. This new event becomes the type of the Business Event that is conveyed to the rule execution inference agent.

Using TIBCO ActiveMatrix BusinessWorks™ for Filtering and Enrichment

When filtering and enhancement activity require access to other components and systems, it may be advantageous to use TIBCO ActiveMatrix BusinessWorks™ for these activities (Figure 13-6). The integration capabilities of ActiveMatrix BusinessWorks can significantly reduce the design time required to implement these functions, and the resulting efficiency is comparable to performing these activities in TIBCO BusinessEvents®.

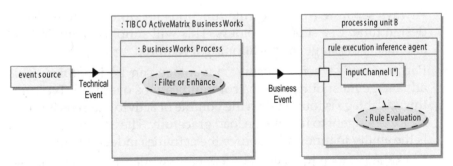

Figure 13-6: *Using TIBCO ActiveMatrix BusinessWorks™ for Filtering and Enhancement*

Partitioning Advantages and Disadvantages

Partitioning provides the following advantages:

- Simplifies maintenance: Changes to one activity are independent of changes to the other.

- Provides deployment flexibility: As long as the rule sets and functions for each activity are separate, changing deployment patterns is a straightforward exercise that can enhance the ability to tune and resource each activity independently.

It should be noted that, in general, stateless activities are easier to partition than stateful activities.

The disadvantages of partitioning are

- Complexity: When activities are deployed in separate agents there is an extra component involved. This can complicate the deployment process and may make traceability a challenge.

- Communications overhead: Deploying the activities in separate components adds communication overhead. This is minimal when both activities are deployed in the same agent, or when both agents are deployed in the same processing unit and a local channel is used for communications.

Partitioning Rules of Thumb

- Always separate rules and rule functions for different activities at design time. Use separate folders. This will simplify maintenance, and it sets the stage for partitioning if required.

- Partition only when a positive advantage can be identified. This advantage must outweigh the communications overhead. Typically, this advantage is found when the volume of activity exceeds the ability for one agent to handle the load gracefully. The advantage gained is the ability to tune and resource the activities independently.

- Consolidate state management. Do not partition the logic required to maintain a concept or its subordinate state machine(s). Doing so will introduce significant locking and coordination problems. For an alternative, see the sequencing challenges discussion in Chapter 14.

Summary

Modularizing complex-event processing solutions is essential for both the comprehensibility and maintainability of the solution. One modularization approach is to separate the logic governing the recognition of a situation from the logic governing what to do once that situation is recognized. Another modularization approach is to separate the filtering and enhancement of events from the subsequent analysis of those events. In both cases an event is used to communicate between the modules.

Modularization provides deployment choices. Both modules can be deployed in a single agent; in two agents running in the same processing unit; or in two agents, each running in separate processing units. This last alternative provides maximum flexibility in tuning and scalability, as additional instances of the processing units can be deployed to add capacity. When filtering and enhancement require integration with other components, there may be advantages to performing these functions in TIBCO ActiveMatrix BusinessWorks.

The best practice is to always modularize the design. This opens the door for deployment flexibility. However, the deployment of the modules in separate agents should only be undertaken if there is a demonstrable benefit.

Chapter 14

Common Design Challenges

Objectives

Complex-event processing solutions often present some significant design challenges. This chapter covers the challenges you are most likely to encounter in your designs. After reading this chapter you will be able to

- Describe how information can be shared
- Describe how locking can be used to maintain data integrity
- Describe the approaches for managing sequencing constraints
- Describe the approaches for managing event duplication

Information Sharing

As soon as a solution is modularized and those modules are deployed in different agents, the problem of sharing information between the modules arises. There are two main approaches for information sharing. One is to use an event to convey the information directly from one module to another. The other is to use the cache as an intermediary.

Using an Event for Information Sharing

The most straightforward means of information sharing is to load the information into an event and send it to the party that requires the information (Figure 14-1).

As simple as this approach is, it has its drawbacks. An event is transient: It lives in the memory of the agent that receives it. If the agent is restarted, the information is gone. The distribution of events is limited: An event delivered to a queue will only be delivered to a single agent.

Using the Cache for Information Sharing

Another approach to information sharing is to use the cache. In this approach, one agent loads the information into a concept that is being managed in Cache Only mode. This results in the concept being placed in the cache, which optionally may have replication and backing store configured to ensure the survivability of the information.

There are two variations on this approach depending on the type of agent consuming the information. Figure 14-2 shows the pattern when

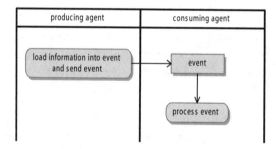

Figure 14-1: *Information Sharing via Event*

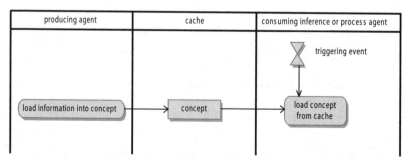

Figure 14-2: *Information Sharing with an Inference or Process Agent via Cache*

the consuming agent is an inference or process agent. The consuming agent is not automatically aware of the cached information: It must explicitly load the concept from the cache. This requires that there be sufficient information in the event triggering the activity in this agent to identify the concept(s) that need to be loaded. This pattern also characterizes the behavior when the consuming agent is a query agent executing a snapshot query.

One potential problem with this pattern arises if the producing agent makes subsequent changes to the concept while the consuming agent is in the process of using the concept. This problem gives rise to the need for locking, which is described later in this chapter.

The pattern is a bit different when the consuming agent is a query agent running a continuous query or a dashboard agent (Figure 14-3). In this situation, the consuming agent is automatically notified when the cached object changes. In the case of the query agent, the object may be a cached event or a concept. In the case of a dashboard agent, the object is a metric. Locking is generally not an issue with this pattern.

A variant on these patterns arises when there are multiple agents that can modify the same concept (Figure 14-4). Here locking is clearly needed to maintain the consistency of the information residing in the concept.

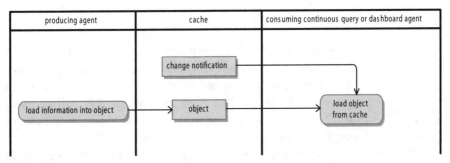

Figure 14-3: *Information Sharing with a Continuous Query or Dashboard Agent via Cache*

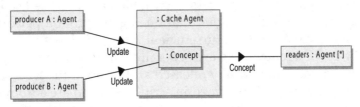

Figure 14-4: *Multiple Producers*

This situation is one that is particularly difficult to manage in practice. Locking not only adds overhead, but also the potential for delays as agents wait for other agents to release their locks. Preferable is an approach in which no more than one agent instance ever updates a particular concept. The patterns described in the section on managing sequencing constraints later in this chapter can be used for this purpose.

A best practice with all these variants is to keep producers distinct from consumers. Mixing both roles in a single agent unnecessarily complicates locking and can lead to serious performance problems.

Locking

Whenever parallel processing is going on there is the potential for conflict when multiple threads attempt to access the same object. The multiple-producers scenario of Figure 14-4 is a good example. When conflicts such as these are unavoidable, locks can be used to manage the situation. A lock ensures that only one thread at a time can access the object.

Locks

Locks in TIBCO BusinessEvents® are not actually locks on the objects themselves—what is actually locked is a value. To make the lock useful, that value must somehow correlate to the object that you want to lock. The recommended best practice is to use the `extID` of the object as the lock value. The `extID` is a value that is specified when the object is created and must be unique across all the objects in the cluster.

There are two possible scopes for a lock: local (within an agent) and global (across all agents). Local locks are used when an object is only being used in one agent, but there are multiple threads within the agent that can use the object. This arises when concurrent RTC is enabled in an inference agent and in process agents. Global locks are used when an object may be used by more than one agent. From a performance perspective, local locks are more efficient than global locks.

In inference agents, locks are generally obtained in a preprocessor function and are automatically released at the end of the RTC cycle. In process agents, locks are obtained in script tasks and are automatically released whenever a checkpoint is performed (see Chapter 8).

Locking Requires Programming Discipline

Because objects are not physically locked, making effective use of locks requires programming discipline. Every thread that requires access to an object requiring locking must obtain a lock. All it takes is one omission and the locking scheme breaks down. For this reason, it is good practice to clearly identify objects that require locking in their description and in accompanying design documentation.

Avoiding Deadlocks

A deadlock can arise when two agents are each waiting for a lock that is presently being held by the other. Here is an example.

- Agent X has locked object A and is trying to lock object B; meanwhile,
- Agent Y has locked object B and is trying to lock object A.

This situation is commonly referred to as a deadly embrace. There are three approaches for dealing with this situation, all of which should be routinely employed.

- If there is a natural hierarchy to the objects, lock in top-to-bottom order.
- Before locking, obtain the `extID` of all objects that require locking. Sort the `extID` list with the primary sort using the object hierarchy and the secondary sort using the values of the `extID`. After the sort, obtain locks in the sort order. This minimizes the likelihood of a deadly embrace.
- Always use a timeout on the lock call, and provide exception handling for the timeout scenario.

Locking and Data Structures

The design of concept data structures can have a significant impact on the complexity of locking. Consider a shipping application in which packages are loaded into containers that are, themselves, loaded onto planes. Two possible data (concept) structures for representing packages, containers, and planes are shown in Figure 14-5. The natural structure is the one that arises from a classical object-oriented modeling approach, and it is the one most people would consider to be representative of the situation.

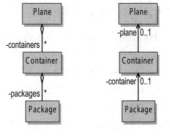

(a) Natural Structure   (b) Inverted Structure

Figure 14-5: *Data Structure Design Alternatives*

However, from a locking perspective, the natural structure has problems. Consider the state of the application when containers are being loaded and unloaded from planes, and when packages are being loaded and unloaded from containers. To ensure data consistency, the parent object must be locked while the child objects are being added and removed.

With this in mind, consider the situation when a large number of planes are being simultaneously loaded or unloaded and when a large number of packages are similarly being added to or removed from containers. A stream of events is generated, each indicating the addition or removal of a package from a container or a container from a plane. The stream of events is sufficiently large that multiple inference agents are required to process the events, with the goal of maintaining a record of where each package and container is presently located. The locking requirements associated with the natural structure will have a significant impact on performance.

Now consider the alternative inverted structure. Each package has a pointer to the container in which it currently resides. Each container has a pointer to the plane in which it currently resides. From a locking perspective, the only lock that is required is for the object whose location is currently being changed. Locking is significantly simpler.

Of course, there is no free lunch here. Obtaining the list of the packages in a container is simple in the natural structure: It is part of the Container data structure. Obtaining the list from the inverted structure requires a query executed by a query agent.

As with many design decisions in complex-event processing, the choice is a trade-off. In this case, the trade-off is between efficiency in editing the data structure versus efficiency in querying the data structure. A thorough understanding of the uses—and the rate of use—of the data is required to make the right choice.

Load Distribution

For both availability and performance reasons, there will be situations in which you need to distribute the workload across multiple instances of the same class of agent. There are several patterns that can be used for this purpose. The choice of distribution pattern depends on the selection of the transport protocol.

Using IP Redirectors to Distribute Load

A common way to distribute load whose requests are being sent using a network-based protocol (e.g., TCP/IP) is to use an IP redirector (Figure 14-6). This is commonly done for HTTP and SOAP over HTTP requests. The IP redirector has a list of candidate service providers to which incoming requests can be directed. Some IP redirectors have mechanisms for determining the workload and status of the service providers, and they use this information when forwarding requests.

Using JMS Queues to Distribute Load

Another common approach to distributing load is to send requests via a Java Message Service (JMS) queue (Figure 14-7). JMS queues deliver each message to exactly one subscriber, in this case one of the service providers. If you are using TIBCO Enterprise Message Service™ as your JMS server, you need to make sure that the exclusive property for the queue is not set.

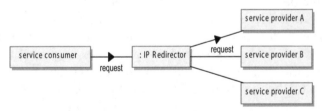

Figure 14-6: *Using an IP Redirector to Distribute Load*

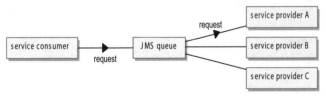

Figure 14-7: *Using JMS Queues to Distribute Load*

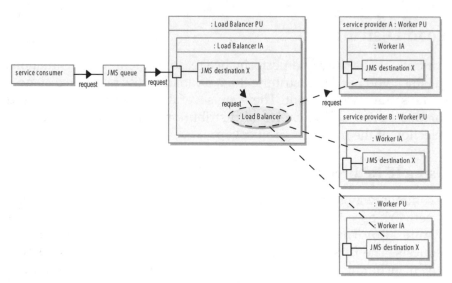

Figure 14-8: *Using TIBCO BusinessEvents® Load Balancer to Distribute Load*

Using TIBCO BusinessEvents® Load Balancer to Distribute Load

An alternative to basic JMS queue load distribution is the use of the TIBCO BusinessEvents load balancer to distribute the load (Figure 14-8). In this pattern there are two types of inference agents: `Load Balancer IA` and `Worker IA`. Both are configured with the identical channel and JMS destination configurations. Each agent is deployed in a separate processing unit.

The `Load Balancer IA` subscribes to the queue and receives events. For each event, it selects a target `Worker IA` and delivers the event to the target worker's destination using a behind-the-scenes TCP transport. From the `Worker IA` perspective, it appears exactly as if the channel had received the event and placed it in the destination.

With no further configuration, the behavior is about the same as if each of the `Worker IA` agents subscribed directly to the queue. However, as you shall see in the next section, there are additional capabilities in the load balancer.

Directing Related Work to a Single Agent

From both a design simplicity and performance perspective, there are advantages to keeping work related to a particular concept instance consolidated in a single agent while simultaneously distributing the work across multiple agents. For example, while distributing work related to bank accounts across many agents, you might want to ensure that all the work related to a particular account executes in a single agent. One of the principal advantages is that since all work related to an instance occurs in the one agent, locking can be local and therefore more efficient. In general, this is the preferred approach for managing any stateful object, especially state machines.

TIBCO BusinessEvents provides a mechanism for realizing this type of load distribution: content-aware load balancing. This is a variation on the load balancing shown in Figure 14-8. The load-balancing configuration not only specifies the routing and worker inference agents, but also a property of the event to be used in directing the event to the workers. The load balancer ensures that all events with the same property value (e.g., the account number) are sent to the same worker.

You may encounter situations in which the incoming event does not contain the precise value you want to use to govern the distribution. In such cases you can specify a preprocessor function that computes the value and assigns it to a property of the event. Other than this type of preprocessor function, the `Load Balancer IA` has no business logic. The `Worker IA` agents execute all the logic needed to process the event.

Managing Sequencing

Many applications present situations in which it is important to maintain the order in which things are done. If you are performing transactions on a bank account, for example, it is important that the deposits and withdrawals actually be executed in the same sequence in which they were initiated.

Sequencing becomes a challenge when there are multiple parties doing the work in parallel (Figure 14-9). Despite the fact that the `source` sends `request 1` before `request 2`, in the absence of any coordination there is no guarantee that `result 1` will be produced before `result 2`. So the question becomes how to preserve sequencing when taking advantage of parallel processing.

This question breaks down into two sub-questions: how to preserve sequencing within a single worker when the worker internally uses parallel processing, and how to preserve sequencing when there are multiple workers. These questions are addressed in *Architecting Composite Applications and Services with TIBCO®* when TIBCO Active

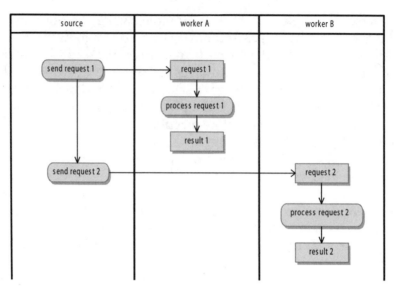

Figure 14-9: *The Sequencing Problem*

Matrix® Service Grid components (including TIBCO Active Matrix BusinessWorks™) play the roles of the worker. Let's take a look at how these questions are addressed when an inference agent is the worker.

Preserving Sequencing within One Inference Agent

By default, preprocessing in an inference agent uses a shared pool of threads. This default configuration is inherently parallel and cannot preserve sequencing. In order to preserve sequencing within the inference agent, two things are necessary.

1. Use a JMS queue (and corresponding JMS destination) for delivering requests. JMS guarantees that, between a single publisher and a single subscriber, messages will be delivered in the order sent.

2. In the configuration of the JMS destination in the CDD, select the Caller's Thread threading model. For JMS destinations, there is a single thread handling input messages, and this choice selects that thread for doing both the preprocessing and the RTC cycle execution.

These choices, together, ensure that an inference agent will preserve sequencing while processing requests.

Preserving Sequencing across Multiple Inference Agents

To ensure sequential processing, you need to use the content-aware load balancing described earlier in this chapter along with some additional configuration requirements.

- Use a JMS queue (and corresponding JMS destination) for delivering requests. JMS guarantees that, between a single publisher and a single subscriber, messages will be delivered in the order sent.

- Use an inference agent configured as a router. In the configuration of its JMS destination in the CDD, select the `Caller's Thread` threading model. For JMS destinations, there is a single thread handling input messages, and this choice ensures that the preprocessing (which does the routing) will be single threaded.

- For each worker inference configuration of the JMS destination in the CDD, select the `Caller's Thread` threading model. For JMS destinations, there is a single thread handling input messages, and this choice selects that thread for doing both the preprocessing and the RTC cycle execution.

Recovering Temporal Sequencing (Reordering)

This situation arises when you have events arriving at a destination out of sequence and you wish to restore the original sequence. Be aware that this is fundamentally a hard problem, one for which there is no generic solution.

The hardest part of this problem lies in knowing when you have received all of the relevant events. Even if you have one distinguished event that is supposed to be last in the sequence, if it arrives out of sequence you will not realize that there are other events still in the pipeline. You can't even begin to address the problem unless you have a working approach for this.

If you are using timestamps in the events as the basis for establishing the sequencing, there is another challenge you may encounter: clock skew. This problem arises when the timestamps are generated by different machines. Keeping clocks synchronized on multiple machines is a notoriously difficult problem. The resulting error, known as clock skew, will produce errors in the timestamps which, in turn, will produce errors in the sequencing.

One common strategy is to not even attempt the sequence restoration; instead, throw away all but the most recent event. When using this approach, the event should contain complete state information (e.g., the current balance or the current inventory level) as opposed to the change in state (e.g., the transaction amount or the change in inventory level). With complete state information, the process is self-healing: Even if there is an error, the next event will correct the situation.

Handling Duplicate Events

When JMS is used as a transport, the inadvertent shutdown of an agent processing a JMS-delivered event will result in the redelivery of that event. If there is only one agent subscribed to the queue, the event will be redelivered when the agent restarts. If there are multiple agents subscribed, the event will immediately be delivered to one of the remaining agents.

Given this, you need to consider what the impact is on your design. If all of the activities being executed as a consequence of the event can be repeated again and again, always producing the same result (these are known as *idempotent* activities), then there is no problem. But if you have activities that are not idempotent (a database insert is one example), then your design must take the possibility of redelivery into account.

One activity that is not idempotent is the creation of an object with a particular `extID`. By default, a check for duplicates is performed within the agent attempting to create the object, but the checking does not extend beyond the agent. By checking the Check for Duplicates box in the agent configuration in the CDD, this check is extended to the entire cluster. However, there is a performance impact that must be considered.

The first step in dealing with non-idempotent activities is recognizing that a redelivery is in progress. JMS provides a mechanism for recognizing that a message is being redelivered, the JMSRedelivery property. However, this property will not be available in TIBCO BusinessEvents unless you explicitly define a JMSRedelivery property on the event to make that information available.

Beyond recognizing that a redelivery is in progress, the logic of what needs to be done depends almost entirely on the nature of the work being done. In general, the approach is as follows:

- Recognize that a redelivery has occurred.
- For each non-idempotent activity:
  - Query to determine whether the activity previously completed.
  - Take appropriate alternate action if needed (e.g., suppress the creation of an object).

Summary

Information can be shared between agents either directly, using events, or indirectly using objects in the cache. If the cache is used, inference and process agents must explicitly retrieve the information from the cache. This retrieval must be triggered by an event and that event must contain sufficient information to identify the object(s) that must be retrieved.

When multiple agents are sharing information in the cache, locking must be used to ensure data integrity. Locks are logical: What is locked is an identifier that corresponds to the object being locked, typically the object's `extID`. Local locks can be used if the design ensures that the object being locked can only be present in the local agent; otherwise, global locks must be used.

One mechanism for ensuring that objects are only present in a single agent is to distribute load in such a way that all the work involving a given object is always sent to the same agent. Content-aware load distribution can be used for this purpose.

In some situations it may be important to process events in the order in which they are received. Within an inference agent, this can be accomplished by using a JMS queue and the Caller's Thread to process the event. This makes the agent single-threaded with respect to that queue. When multiple agents are involved, content-aware load distribution must also be employed.

The use of JMS queues can result in the duplicate delivery of events when agents are shut down unexpectedly. Duplicate delivery can be detected by adding a JMSRedelivery property to the event. If there are non-idempotent activities being performed, logic must be added in the event of redelivery to determine whether the activity was previously completed and to take appropriate alternate actions.

Part IV

Deployment

Chapter 15

Case Study: Nouveau Health Care

Objectives

One of the challenges in writing about architecture and architecture patterns is to pick examples that are rich enough to motivate the discussion and realistic enough to represent real-world challenges while at the same time being simple enough to be readily explained.

The fictional Nouveau Health Care case study was created for this purpose. Its business processes, though simplified when compared with their real-world equivalent, are still complex enough to present most of the common design challenges found in their real-world counterparts. An important aspect of reality is that the processes and their corresponding solution implementations do not operate in isolation; rather, they interact with one another and with other business processes as they would in the real world.

Different aspects of the Nouveau Health Care example are used throughout this architecture book series. This chapter provides a conceptual overview of the company and its business processes, and then introduces the Claim Tracker and its related business processes, which are used to illustrate many of the points and design principles in this book.

After reading this chapter you will be able to describe the Claim Tracker requirements and architecture.

Nouveau Health Care Solution Architecture

Nouveau Health Care is a traditional health care insurance company. It sells health care insurance policies and covers claim payments with the revenue it collects from its premiums. It also administers the processing of claims.

There are factors that add to the complexity of Nouveau's business. In some cases, the employers for whom Nouveau provides the health care benefits also provide the funds for paying the claims: Nouveau simply administers the policies. In other cases, the administration of specialized services (vision and dental care) is farmed out to other companies. Both variations present some interesting design challenges.

Nouveau Health Care Business Processes

Our use of Nouveau focuses on four of its business processes (Figure 15-1):

1. Validate Membership and its underlying Validate Membership Service

2. Manage Payments, which manages claim payments to health care service providers

3. Process Claim, and its initiator, Route Claim, which together handle the processing of insurance claims

4. Monitor Claim Processing, a process that monitors the execution of claim processing

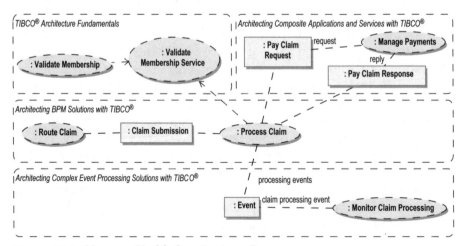

Figure 15-1: *Nouveau Health Care Business Processes*

The Validate Membership process is used by authorized parties (health care providers, employers, and members) to validate whether or not an individual was covered by the policy on a given date. This business process uses an underlying Validate Membership Service, which is also used by the Process Claim business process. Validate Membership is used as an example in the *TIBCO® Architecture Fundamentals* book.

The Manage Payments process manages the payments to health care service providers resulting from health care claims.[1] What makes this process interesting is that, under normal circumstances, payments are made on a periodic basis (e.g., monthly) to health care service providers. This means that the payment manager must keep track of pending payments. By exception, payments to health care service providers for specific claims may be made immediately. The design of this process is explored in *Architecting Composite Applications and Services with TIBCO®*.

Process Claim and its related Route Claim process actually handle the processing of health care claims. Routing is required because some claims are processed by Nouveau itself while others are processed by partner companies. Process Claim is a consumer of both the Validate Membership Service and the services of the Payment Manager. Process Claim and Route Claim are used as examples in the upcoming book, *Architecting BPM Solutions with TIBCO®*.

Monitor Claim Processing keeps track of the progress of claim processing. This is necessary because some claim processing is done by partner companies. Monitoring provides uniform tracking of all health care claims regardless of whether Nouveau or one of its partners is handling the claim. This process is used as an example in this book.

Nouveau Health Care Architecture Pattern

The business processes of Nouveau Health Care are executed by a collection of components (Figure 15-2). The Claim Router provides an interface for the Billing Provider to submit claims. It validates membership with the Membership Service, routes claims to the Claim Processor, and reports status to the Claim Tracker. The Claim Processor (and there may be more than one) adjudicates the claim, validating membership via the Membership Service, requesting claim payment via the Payment Manager, and reporting status to the Claim Tracker.

---

1. In the real world, the Manage Payments process would also manage payments to members, reimbursing them for claim-related expenses that they have already paid themselves.

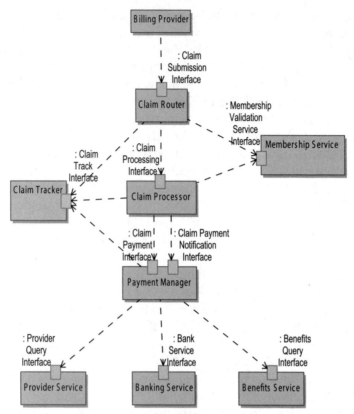

Figure 15-2: *Nouveau Health Care Architecture Pattern for Claim Processing*

The Payment Manager pays the service providers, getting the account associated with the plan from the Benefits Service, the account associated with the health care service provider from the Provider Service, and using the Banking Service to make the payments. It also reports status to the Claim Tracker.

Nouveau Health Care in Context

Nouveau Health Care is part of a larger environment that includes the health care service providers that submit claims and the partner companies that process some of the claims (Figure 15-3). Here we see that there can be more than one claim processor, which explains the need for the Claim Router.

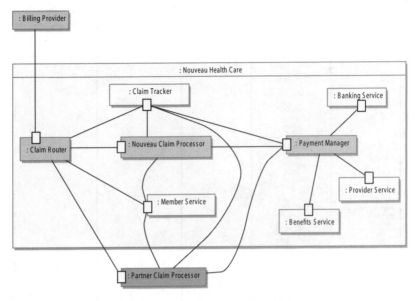

Figure 15-3: *Nouveau Health Care Claim Processing in Context*

Processing Claims from Providers

Health care claims can be submitted by either the health care service provider or by the member to whom the service was provided. In the Nouveau Health Care example we focus on the claims submitted by providers and on the payments to those providers.

Figure 15-4 presents an overview of the processing of claims submitted by health care service providers. This sunny-day scenario shows provider interactions via the U.S. quasi-standard HIPAA transactions[2] and shows deferred payments to the provider. The process model shows payer and provider account references, but not the details of the interactions with the Benefits Service and Provider Service required to obtain them. Similarly, it shows where membership is validated, but not the interactions with the Member Service that actually does the validation. Finally, for simplicity, all interactions with the Claim Tracker have been omitted.

---

2. In practice, each HIPAA transaction interface that is implemented by an enterprise is extended to accommodate the specific requirements of that enterprise.

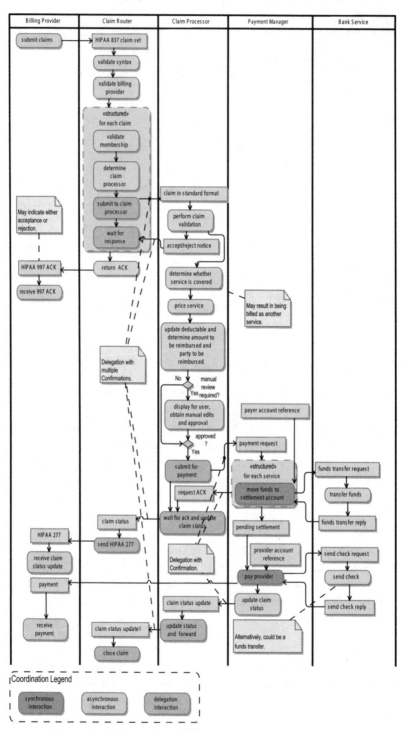

Figure 15-4: *Processing Claims from Providers*

Claim Tracker

The `Claim Tracker` is an example of a Track-and-Trace solution as described in Chapter 3. There are at least three processes associated with the `Claim Tracker` (Figure 15-5). The obvious process is `Monitor Claim Processing`—after all, that's the whole point of the `Claim Tracker`. But monitoring doesn't do any good if the resulting `Claim Status` is not made available to other participants. Thus a secondary process, `Obtain Claim Status`, is also required. However, even this is not enough. If the `Claim Tracker` determines that the process is not executing properly, it is best to proactively send a notification of the exception. This implies that there is yet a third process, `Resolve Claim Processing Exception`.

While it may be obvious that the `Claim Tracker` is responsible for `Monitor Claim Processing` and `Obtain Claim Status`, it should be equally obvious that the tracker is not going to resolve the problems leading to the exception. Figure 15-6 shows the configuration of the `Claim Tracker`, clarifying the communications channels and indicating that the exception-resolver role is being played by a person and some as-yet unspecified interface.

This design assumes that the claim processing participants are providing the requisite `Claim Status Notifications`. The next section will explore in more detail what notification is required and what information is retained in the `Claim Status`.

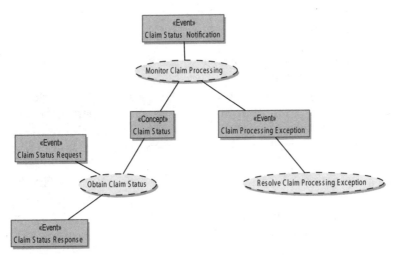

Figure 15-5: *Claim Tracking Processes*

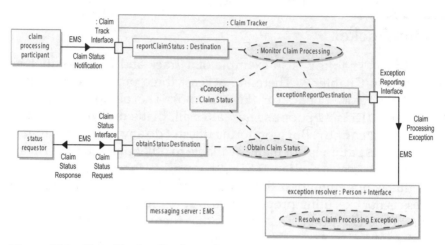

Figure 15-6: *Claim Tracker Configuration*

Although we are not going to explore the exception-resolver role here, in practice it is very important to explore this role, for several reasons. Exploring the role will clarify the information that must be either present in the exception event or available via other interfaces in order to diagnose and fix the problem. Some of those interfaces may not exist! Furthermore, the interfaces required to take corrective action may not exist either! Exploring exception resolution will help you discover additional interfaces that will be required, and understand better the true scope of the project.

Claim Status Concept

For any track and trace solution, a key task is to identify the important states of the item being tracked. The states are best thought of as milestones in the process being tracked. This will help you identify the appropriate level of detail. Figure 15-7 shows the state machine for claim tracking. The states represent the milestones. The transitions are labeled with the status being reported in the `Claim Status Notification` event.

Of course, this is just the sunny-day scenario. The most likely scenario for process breakdown is that the process simply gets stuck in a particular state. To detect this kind of breakdown, add SLA timers that start when each state is entered (Figure 15-8).

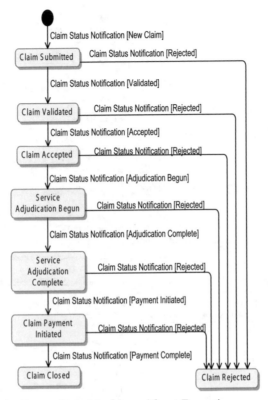

Figure 15-7: *Claim Status State Machine without Exceptions*

Beyond the simple state of the claim processing, additional information is required to monitor the claim (Figure 15-9). This includes the identifier of the claim (which should also be the concept's extID), the date submitted, and a list of the status reports that have been submitted against the claim.

Claim Track Interface

The Claim Track Interface is shown in Figure 15-10, along with the enumeration of allowed values for the status being reported.

The Claim Status Interface is shown in Figure 15-11. In reality, it is likely that more information would be desired in the Claim Status Response. In order to understand these requirements, the use of this interface in various processes should be explored.

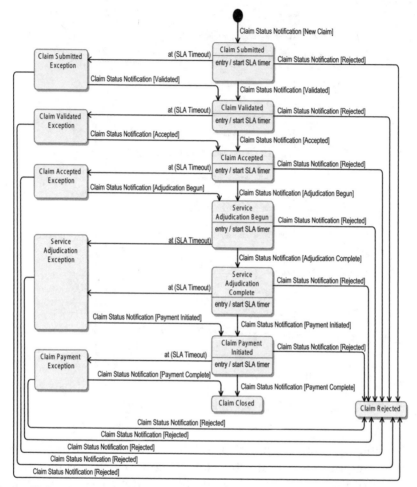

Figure 15-8:

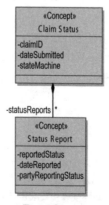

Figure 15-9: *Claim Status Concept Data Structure*

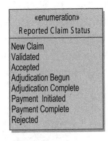

Figure 15-10: *Claim Track Interface*

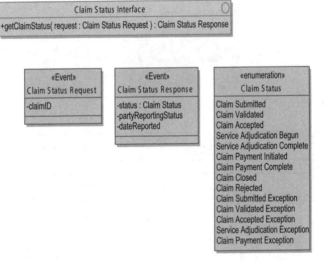

Figure 15-11: *Claim Status Interface*

The Exception Reporting Interface is shown in Figure 15-12. It is likely that more information would be desired in this response. To understand these requirements, the Resolve Claim Processing Exception process should be explored in more detail.

Claim Tracker Processes

The Claim Tracker executes two processes: Monitor Claim Processing and Obtain Claim Status.

Monitor Claim Processing

Figure 15-13 shows the processing of a Claim Status Notification event. This processing assumes that the Claim Status concept has a state machine configured as per Figure 15-8. The RTC cycle will evaluate the transitions of the state machine.

Figure 15-14 shows the behavior that occurs when an SLA timer expires. Since there is no channel and destination associated with the event, the preprocessor function must be specially registered using the `Cluster.registerStateMachineTimeoutCallback()` catalog function.

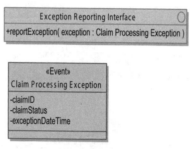

Figure 15-12: *Exception Reporting Interface*

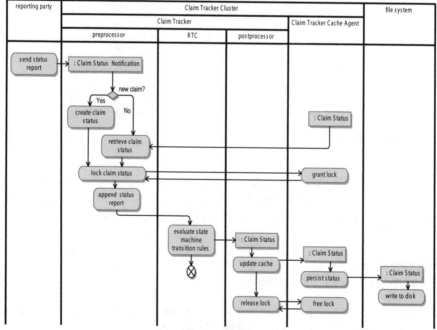

Figure 15-13: *Monitor Claim Processing Behavior*

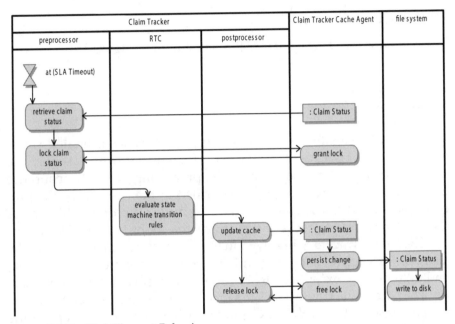

Figure 15-14: *SLA Timeout Behavior*

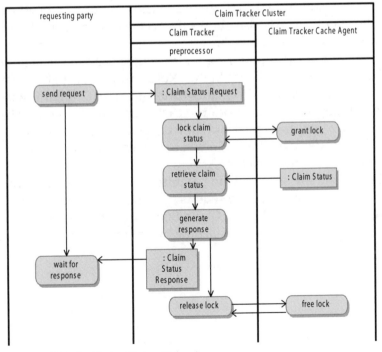

Figure 15-15: *Obtain Claim Status Behavior*

Obtain Claim Status

The behavior for Obtain Claim Status is shown in Figure 15-15.

Summary

The Nouveau Health Care case study provides a coordinated set of example problems across the TIBCO Press architecture book series. The primary focus of the case study is the processing of health insurance claims. With the business model described in the case study, the processing of claims can be distributed across multiple parties. This creates the need for a Claim Tracker to centralize the status tracking for claims.

The Claim Tracker is involved in three processes: (1) monitoring the claim processing, (2) obtaining and returning claim status upon request, and (3) reporting exceptions to a process that resolves the exceptions.

The core of the Claim Tracker functionality is represented by a state machine associated with the Claim Status concept that is kept in the cache. This state machine shows the expected milestones of normal claim processing as well as exception states that are entered when service-level agreements are violated. Violations of these service-level agreements result in a `Claim Processing Exception` event being sent. The state machine also shows the recovery actions that are possible once an exception has occurred.

Since most of the monitoring logic is embedded in the state machine, the processing of a Claim Status Notification is straightforward. If it is a new claim, the Claim Status concept is created. Otherwise, the existing status is retrieved from the cache. In either case, the object is locked and a Status Report appended containing the details of the report. The RTC cycle is then allowed to process the event and drive the transitions in the state machine.

Timeouts in the state machine require their associated preprocessor functions to be specially registered. As with the normal processing, timeouts require the retrieval of the Claim Status from the cache and locking it prior to evaluating the state machine transitions in the RTC cycle.

Chapter 16

Performance

Objectives

Having the right functional capabilities doesn't do you any good if your solution can't meet the performance requirements. This chapter explores the design choices that impact performance, the tuning mechanisms available in TIBCO BusinessEvents®, and describes an approach to performance estimation. It concludes with some sizing rules of thumb that can be used in the absence of any detailed information. After reading this chapter you will be able to

- Describe how the profiler can be used to obtain RTC performance data
- Describe how design choices impact agent performance
- Explain how to perform a demand analysis
- List some rule-of-thumb sizing guidelines for development environments

TIBCO BusinessEvents® Profiler

TIBCO BusinessEvents® contains a profiler that gives you performance information about the execution of the RTC cycle. This information can be used not only to understand where time is being spent, but also to compare the performance profiles of different rule designs.

There are several ways in which the profiler can be turned on and off. These include the following:

- TIBCO BusinessEvents Monitoring and Management: This application provides an interactive mechanism for turning profiling on and off.

- Agent properties: The `be.engine.profile...` family of properties can be used to statically configure profiling. These properties are applied when the agent starts.

- TIBCO Hawk®: Each agent has an embedded Hawk microagent interface that includes operations for turning profiling on and off. The Hawk console can be used to interactively control profiling, or Hawk rules can be written to turn profiling on and off when specific conditions exist.

- Catalog functions: Catalog functions are provided that turn profiling on and off. These can be incorporated into preprocessor functions or rule actions.

Profiling is an essential tool for understanding the performance implications of your design. However, just turning the profiler on will not necessarily provide you with the information you require. Many performance issues will not be apparent unless there are a significant number of objects in the memory and/or cache. You need to analyze your solution and determine the worst-case peak-condition number of objects, and then observe the behavior under those conditions. This may require a special test to simulate those conditions.

Design Choices and Agent Performance

There are a number of design choices that can impact performance, including

- Structuring rule conditions
- Organizing decision tables
- Accessing large XML event payloads
- Locking objects
- Choosing threading models
- Using synchronous I/O calls in rule actions

Structuring Rule Conditions

There are three basic types of rule conditions: filters, equivalent joins, and nonequivalent joins. Filters are comparisons of object properties against fixed values. Filter operations consume minimal resources. An example is:

```
transaction.amount <= 5.00;
```

Equivalent joins compare values from two objects using an equality operator. The fact that a join is being performed makes it computationally more expensive than a simple filter operation, but the operator being used for comparison is relatively efficient. An example is:

```
transaction.accountNumber == account.accountNumber;
```

Nonequivalent joins compare values from two objects using an inequality operator. This is the least efficient type of condition. An example is:

```
transactionA.amount < transactionB.amount;
```

When you compile your project, creating an EAR file, TIBCO BusinessEvents sorts the conditions so that filter conditions are performed first, followed by equivalent joins, and then nonequivalent joins. However, there is no sorting performed within each of these categories: The conditions are evaluated in the order in which they appear in the rule definition.

If you perceive that one condition will be more efficient than another, you should order the clauses accordingly. This is so important that if you have multiple equivalent joins in a rule, you will receive a log file warning that there are multiple equivalent joins in the rule. The warning is intended as a reminder that you need to carefully consider the ordering. This is a situation in which the use of the profiler is highly recommended—it will give you better insight as to what is actually going on in the RTC cycle.

Beyond simply ordering the clauses, you have design choices in structuring your rule conditions. The normal best practice is to keep each type of condition separate, on its own line with a semicolon at the end. If you do this, the compiler will sort the conditions as described above. However, you have the option of combining clauses into larger expressions. This is commonly employed as a means of handling null values:

```
Account.tinyTransaction != null && Account.tinyTransaction.
amount < 5.00;
```

If you place multiple clauses in an expression, the clauses will be evaluated in the order specified. But be careful when you build compound expressions: You may be forcing a less-efficient evaluation. See Listing 5-2 for an example of such an inefficient design.

Organizing Decision Tables

Decision tables are compiled into a decision tree that is used at runtime to compute the return values. This tree can be visualized in the TIBCO BusinessEvents® Studio. The tree will show you the order in which conditions are going to be evaluated. As with rule conditions, you want to organize your decision table so that filter conditions are evaluated before equivalent joins and equivalent joins are evaluated before non-equivalent joins. Exactly the same considerations apply as with rule conditions.

Sometimes you will encounter situations in which performance will be better if you split a decision table into two or more tables. A common situation is one in which some of the input data fields are used to compute a score or ranking, and the result of this computation is used as part of the logic for the rest of the decision table. In such cases, execution will often be more efficient if the scoring is factored into one decision, and then the scoring result is fed to another decision table that makes the final decision (Figure 16-1).

Accessing Large XML Event Payloads

When a value in an XML event payload is accessed in a rule condition, an XPath expression is used to identify the value. This expression must be evaluated in order to obtain the value, and it is evaluated once for each appearance of the value in a conditional expression. Furthermore, the cost of this evaluation increases with the depth of the nesting in the XML data structure.

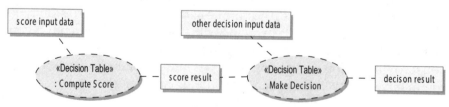

Figure 16-1: *Factoring Decision Tables*

When a particular value is accessed frequently, there may be benefits in adding a property to the event specifically to lessen the cost of accessing the value. A preprocessor function can be used to compute the value of the property at the time the event is created. With this approach, the cost of accessing the value in the XML structure is incurred once, and the value is now in a location where it can be accessed at minimal cost.

Locking Objects

Whenever a mutable object is used in more than one rule or rule function, locks must be employed to ensure the integrity and consistency of the information in the object. Recall that locks can be either local to one agent or global across multiple agents, with local locks being more efficient than global locks.

The placement of rules and rule functions will determine the type of locking required. If your design ensures that a given object will be accessed only by a single instance of an agent, then you can safely use local locking and gain the resulting efficiency. On the other hand, if you cannot guarantee that the object will only be accessed by one agent instance, you have no choice other than to use global locks.

Global locking carries with it a performance penalty. Often the need for global locking arises when multiple agents of the same type are deployed to distribute the load. The goal is to increase capacity, but the added overhead of global locking can significantly detract from the expected gains. This is a situation in which content-aware load balancing (discussed in Chapter 14) can be employed to direct work to agents in such a way that local locks will provide adequate protection.

Choosing Inference Agent Threading Models

There are three choices you have to make with regard to inference agent threading: pre-RTC, RTC, and post-RTC. Each choice has its own performance implications.

Pre-RTC Choices

Each destination specifies the threads to be used in processing the events that arrive at the destination. These are the threads that not only perform the preprocessor functions, but also execute the RTC cycle that follows. There are three choices:

1. Shared pool threads (the default)
2. Dedicated worker thread pool
3. Caller thread

The shared pool is shared across all destinations that select this option. At peak periods, events arriving at different destinations may compete for these threads. While convenient, this option does not guarantee the availability of threads to process inputs from a given destination.

The dedicated worker thread pool is specific to the destination. Creating a dedicated pool guarantees the availability of threads to process events arriving at the destination. However, this approach is not magic. There are practical limitations on the number of threads a given Java virtual machine (JVM) can effectively support. This limit varies depending upon the hardware being used and the manufacturer of the JVM. In high-performance situations, some research and/or experimentation are warranted to understand these practical limits.

The third option, caller thread, uses the thread that actually received the event for all of the preprocessing and RTC execution activities. The number of caller threads varies, depending upon the channel transport being used. Many of the channel callers, such as HTTP and TCP, are multi-threaded. Others, specifically the JMS channel, are single threaded. The use of the caller thread for JMS channels is a way of ensuring that the associated preprocessing and RTC execution is single threaded. This can be important when sequencing is a requirement.

Just because you choose a threading model that has multiple threads does not necessarily mean that all of these threads are going to be actively processing inputs. Threads may be blocked for a variety of reasons: making synchronous I/O calls, waiting for object locks, or waiting to execute the RTC cycle if RTC is configured to be single threaded. All of this needs to be considered when choosing the threading model and determining the size of the thread pools.

RTC Choices

There are two threading choices for RTC: single-threaded (the default) or concurrent. Choosing the concurrent option creates a situation in which multiple Rete networks (each running in a different thread) may be operating on the same working memory contents. Changes made by one network may alter the course of another's execution. Locking is generally required to ensure deterministic execution of the rule logic.

Given this, it is tempting to fall back on the single-threaded option as a shortcut to avoid the need for locking. However, making this choice assumes that the objects in working memory are not in use in other agents. In particular, you are making the assumption that you will never have to deploy more than one instance of the agent; as soon as you do, locking again becomes an issue.

The best practice here is not to use single threading arbitrarily as a means for avoiding locking. Do your analysis and lock accordingly. If you choose not to lock, make sure the resulting deployment constraint is clear: There can never be more than one instance of this agent deployed.

Post-RTC Choices

If cache-aside backing store is being used, there is a threading choice to be made for post-RTC processing: single-threaded or parallel processing. With single threading, all of the post-RTC work is performed in a single thread (see Figure 5-22 for details). With parallel processing, database and cache updates happen independently (see Figure 5-23).

Aside from just being a performance-related tuning option, this choice also impacts the possibility of data inconsistency in the event of unexpected component shutdown or communications interruption. In the single-threaded model, all database updates are performed prior to updating the cache. Any information that appears in the cache is guaranteed to have been persisted. This is not the case for parallel processing since the cache updates happen independent of database updates.

Using Synchronous I/O Calls in Rule Actions

Synchronous calls provide confirmation that external work has been performed. This information is often useful in structuring the logic governing the execution of actions. For this reason, it is tempting to use these calls in the action part of a rule. However, you need to seriously consider the performance implications: The thread making the call will be blocked until the I/O completes. If RTC is configured single threaded, then all RTC activity is halted until the I/O has completed. Be sure you consider the performance implications before deciding to go this route!

Demand Analysis

Event-driven processes (Figure 16-2) follow a pattern: Some triggering event begins a daisy-chain of interactions between components. Eventually the activity dies down until the next triggering event occurs. Once the triggering events are identified and the consequent component interaction patterns are understood, determining the demand that will be placed on each component is relatively straightforward.

The process for analyzing the demand breaks down as follows.

- Identify the triggering events. These are, for the most part, external events, but timer events also qualify as triggering events. Determine the peak rate at which each triggering event occurs. Secondarily, determine whether these peaks occur at the same or different times.

- Determine the component interaction pattern that results from each triggering event. These should already have been documented as part of the solution architecture.

- Determine the rates at which non-triggering events in the interaction pattern occur relative to the triggering event. In some cases this will be 1:1, but in other cases a single triggering event will either conditionally result in a non-triggering event or will result in multiple non-triggering events.

- Determine the rate at which each component must respond to incoming events. Determine whether a single instance of the component will be able to handle the load or whether some form of load distribution is required. This analysis should address not only the computations required, but the data retention as well.

- Determine the load on each communications channel.

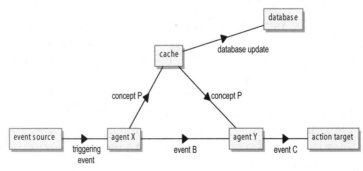

Figure 16-2: *Event-Driven Component Interaction*

The following sections apply this approach to the analysis of the Claim Tracker described in Chapter 15.

Triggering Events

There are three triggering events in the Claim Tracker. Two of these originate externally: `Claim Status Notification` and `Claim Status Request`. The third source of triggering events is the timers associated with the `Claim Status State Machine`. These timers identify overdue claim status events.

Claim Status Notification Rate

Nouveau Health Care has 30 million members under its plan and handles up to 4.4 million claims per day. At peak times, claims will be submitted at a rate of 620 claims/second. The normal processing of a claim will produce seven `Claim Status Notification` events. Six of these result in steps that have service-level agreement (SLA) targets for completion (see Table 16-1).

The notification events for different steps in the process have different arrival patterns. There are two peak periods of activity. During claim submission, all of the states up to Claim Payment Initiated will be traversed in 16 minutes. This means that Claim Status Notification events will be arriving at 3,720 events/second during peak times.

The second peak period occurs at the end of the month when claims are paid. At 4.4 million claims per day, that is 136.4 million claims per month. These payments occur over an eight-hour period,

Table 16-1: *Claim Status Notification Processing Steps*

Step	SLA	Typical delay time
Claim Submitted	5 minutes	1 minute
Claim Accepted	1 hour	5 minutes
Service Adjudication Begun	8 hours	5 minutes
Service Adjudication Complete	1 hour	5 minutes
Claim Payment Initiated	33 days	16 days
Claim Closed	1 hour	5 minutes

with one event occurring each time a payment is completed. This results in an event rate of 4,736 events per second over the four hours. These events always occur at periods of low claim submission activity. Thus, the normal peak rate, for analysis purposes, is 4,736 events/second.

Communication outages may result in additional peaks of activity (more analysis is warranted here). For the purposes of this analysis, we will consider that the capacity to process events at the expected peak rate of 4,736 events/second is adequate, with the full expectation that it will take time for the backlog of status reports to be cleared out. The assumption is that the EMS server will serve as a buffer for absorbing this backlog.

Claim Status Timeout Rate

Noveau expects that 1% of claims will experience an issue resulting in a timeout event. Under normal conditions, the peak rate of these timeouts will follow the same pattern as the notification events, yielding a peak rate of 6.2 claims per second.

Outages, however, may result in significantly higher peak rates. If a communication outage prevents the delivery of notifications, the rate of timeouts may begin to approach the claim submission rate of 620 events/second.

Claim Status Request Rate

Noveau is planning to make claim status information available to the members of its health care plans. It is anticipated that 1% of claims will result in claim status requests. This works out to 44,000 claim status requests per day. In lieu of better information, Noveau is assuming that half of these requests will occur over four hours. This works out to about three requests per second.

From a performance perspective, this rate is so low compared to the status notification events that we will ignore them from a demand analysis perspective.

Analysis

Claim Processing

The component interaction pattern for monitoring claim processing is shown in Figure 15-13. Each step in the claim process results in a corresponding notification event. Six of the steps have associated SLAs and typical delay times relative to the previous event (Table 16-1). Note that there is a significant differential between the SLA for many of the activities and the typical delay time. This is because Nouveau is trying to fully automate the processing of up to 95% of the claims, and the typical times reflect the expected performance for automated claims. The long duration for Claim Payment Initiated reflects the fact that payments are actually made monthly.

Given this information and a peak rate of 4,736 events/second, the following conclusions are reached.

- The Claim Tracker inference agents will receive events at a rate of 4,736 per second.
- Each event will require the cache to both retrieve and update Claim Status objects at a combined rate of 9,472 per second. That's a worst-case combined data rate of 71 MB/second between the inference and cache agents. The cache agent will need to grant and release locks at a combined rate of 9,472 requests/second.
- The file system will write data at a worst-case peak rate of 35.5 MB/second.
- The EMS server will receive messages at the rate of 4,736/second.
- The network bandwidth required will be a combination of the messaging load and the cache-inference agent load. Assuming messages are 1KB in size, the message load is 76 Mb/second. The cache load is 568 Mb/second. Combined load is 644 Mb/second.

Claims must be retained in the Claim Tracker until they are closed. On average, a claim takes 16 days to complete. Thus the Claim Tracker must retain approximately 70.4 million claims. By experiment, it has been determined that a single claim requires 15KB of cache space. Thus the net cache size is 1.056TB.

Timeout Notification

The interaction pattern for timeout notification is shown in Figure 15–14. The peak rate at which timeouts will occur is 620 events/second. The following conclusions are reached.

- The inference agent processing these timeouts will receive events at 620 events/second.
- The cache agent will need to grant and release locks at a combined rate of 1,240 requests/second. It will need to retrieve and update Claim Status objects at a combined rate of 1,240 requests/second.

- The file system will write data at a worst-case peak rate of 9.3 MB/second.

- The EMS message server will receive exception messages at the rate of 620/second.

- The network load will be 5 Mb/second from messaging and 149 Mb/second from the cache, for a total of 154 Mb/second.

Analysis Interpretation

The cache must retain approximately 1TB of data. Worst case, keeping all the data memory resident and assuming each cache agent can manage 64GB of memory, this will require 17 cache agents. Shared-nothing backing store will be used. Further analysis exploring the performance impact of only holding part of the data in memory may indicate that a reduction in the number of cache agents is possible.

The inference agents processing the change notifications need to process 4,736 events/second. A preliminary performance test performed on a laptop (8-core) and simulating the full life cycle of notification events with corresponding state machine updates produced a throughput of 425 events/second. Based on this preliminary analysis, approximately 12 inference agents will be required, along with a load distribution mechanism.

The inference agents processing timeout notifications must process events at a rate of 620 events/second. While no simulation was performed for this activity, using the previous performance test the initial estimate is that two inference agents will be required for this task.

The EMS server will need to handle 5,356 1KB messages/second, which is plausible for a single EMS instance. Attention will need to be paid to the storage configuration to attain this throughput.

The network will need to handle 798 Mb/second. Attention will have to be paid to the network design to ensure the availability of this bandwidth.

These are just preliminary estimates. Performance tests on the actual hardware to be used will be required for more accurate sizing.

Sizing Rules of Thumb

Because of long lead times for acquiring hardware, you may be asked to provide sizing information for development environments without having any indication of the actual application. In such cases, the following rules of thumb can be used:

- Inference agents: 1 to 2 GB RAM per agent
- Query agents: 1 to 2 GB RAM per agent
- Cache agents: 4 to 8 GB RAM per agent

Actual sizing information for production agents will depend heavily on the actual solution being deployed. Query agent memory requirements will depend heavily on the size of the data sets being returned. Cache agent memory sizing will depend on the number of concurrently active objects in the cache and the size of the objects. The lifetime of objects will determine the total size of the cache.

Summary

Your solution must be able to perform in a satisfactory manner for it to be a success. Achieving a satisfactory result requires understanding both the performance requirements and the ability of your design to attain those performance goals.

The profiler provided with TIBCO BusinessEvents is a useful tool for understanding how inference agent rules are being evaluated at runtime. When rules are complicated and there is significant interaction among rules, this tool is indispensable. The information it provides can be used to refine your design to attain better performance.

There are other design decisions that you make that also impact performance. These include

- The manner in which rule conditions are structured
- The manner in which decision tables are structured
- The manner in which large XML event payloads are accessed in rule conditions

- Your choice of locking strategies
- Your choice of threading models for pre-RTC, RTC, and post-RTC processing
- The use of synchronous I/O in rule actions

In order to evaluate your solution's ability to support performance requirements, it is necessary to convert these requirements into an understanding of the demands that they place on individual components. This can be accomplished by

1. Identifying the triggering events and the peak rate at which they occur,

2. Evaluating the pattern of interaction that occurs for each triggering event and determining the resulting impact on each of the components involved, and

3. Given this understanding of demand, determining how many agents of each type will be required to support the demand.

Chapter 17

Deployment Planning

Objectives

When planning the deployment of a complex-event processing solution based on TIBCO BusinessEvents®, there are a number of things that you, the architect, need to define. How should the functionality be modularized? How should objects be managed and persisted? What is your intent regarding the actual deployment of the solution? What are the deployment requirements for supporting run-time configurability? What do you need to consider in terms of monitoring your solution?

This chapter focuses on these issues. After reading this chapter, you will be able to describe what the architect needs to say about the following:

- Modularization
- Object management configuration
- Deployment patterns
- Deployment requirements for run-time configurability
- Monitoring

Modularization

When you modularize a design, you are defining a decomposition of your design into units that are more readily maintained, managed, and tuned. The modularization of your design can be as important as the functionality itself in determining the success of your solution.

Modularization Units

There are three levels of modularization in a TIBCO BusinessEvents® solution (Figure 17-1). At the highest level is the cluster. Each cluster contains one or more processing units, and each processing unit contains one or more agents.

Each solution requires at least one cluster, and some may involve more than one. For example, a solution using both inference agents and process agents must have at least two clusters, since inference agents and process agents cannot be deployed in the same cluster. For performance reasons, a solution in which dashboard agents are being used for visualization should have a separate cluster for the agents involved in managing the visualization (including inference, cache, and dashboard agents). These should be in a cluster separate from the cluster executing the functional part of the solution.

Modularization is largely about the packaging of functionality. It reflects your decisions about where different blocks of functionality

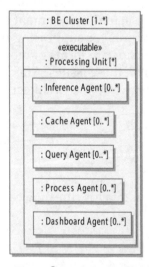

Figure 17-1: *TIBCO BusinessEvents® Modularization Units*

(e.g., rules and rule functions) should be located. How many different types of agents should there be, and what functionality goes in each? How many different types of processing units should there be, and which types of agents go in each processing unit? And, finally, how many clusters are required, and which types of processing units go in each cluster?

There's more to modularization than just packaging decisions. When you place blocks of functionality that need to interact in different modules, you also need to define how these units will interact, and what events and/or concepts need to be exchanged. When events are exchanged, you need to define the channels and destinations that will be used for their delivery.

Agents

In the cluster deployment descriptor for each cluster you define the classes of agents that are available for deployment. The simplest approach to modularization is simply to have one class for each type of agent (inference, cache, query, process, and dashboard). However, this may not be suitable for more complex designs. Performance considerations often warrant a partitioning of functionality, resulting in different classes for some types of agent.

Partitioning keeps one block of functionality from competing with another for the same resources. Generally, when you partition functionality into different classes, the intent is that each class will eventually be deployed in a different processing unit and possibly on a different machine as well. By deploying in this manner, instances of the classes can be scaled and tuned independently.

For example, if you were to employ the partitioning patterns discussed in Chapter 13, you might end up defining three different inference agent classes (Figure 17-2). One of the classes, the Filtering IA, executes the filtering and enrichment logic. A second, the Situation Recognition IA, executes the logic necessary to recognize the situation. A third, the Action IA, executes the logic necessary to determine what actions are required.

Figure 17-2: *Partitioning Functionality across Multiple Inference Agents*

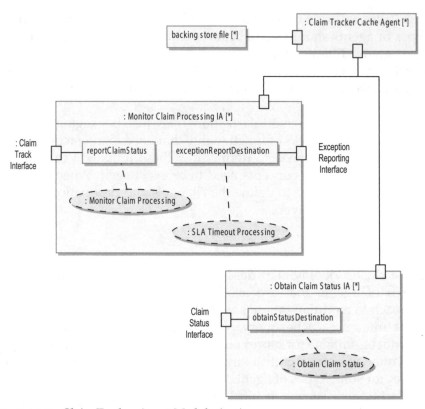

Figure 17-3: *Claim Tracker Agent Modularization*

Figure 17-3 shows the Claim Tracker agent modularization. There are three blocks of functionality: `Monitor Claim Processing`, `SLA Timeout Processing`, and `Obtain Claim Status`. TIBCO BusinessEvents requires that the timeout processing for a state machine be executed in the same inference agents as the normal transition processing, thus the `Monitor Claim Processing` and `SLA Timeout Processing` are co-located in the `Monitor Claim Processing IA`.

As was determined in Chapter 16, initial estimates are that the solution will require twelve agents to support `Monitor Claim Processing` and two to support `SLA Timeout Processing`, so a total of fourteen `Monitor Claim Processing IA` agents will be required. Seventeen `Claim Tracker Cache Agents` will be required, each with its own backing store file. A single `Obtain Claim Status IA` agent is needed.

Processing Units

Processing units are the engines of a TIBCO BusinessEvents solution. Some decisions about how many types of processing units to have in a

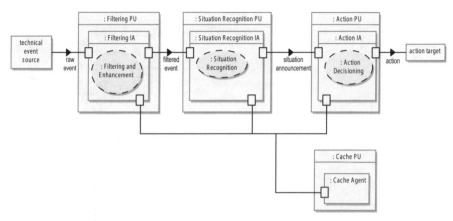

Figure 17-4: *Processing Unit Modularization Example*

design are driven by technical constraints. A processing unit that hosts a cache agent, for example, cannot host more than one cache agent and may not host any other type of agent.

Further partitioning of agents into processing units is generally driven by performance considerations. While there is a lot of tuning capability in each agent, there is a practical limitation as to how much can be done in a processing unit, which is just a JVM.

Figure 17-4 shows the processing unit modularization for the Claim Tracker example. Note that each processing unit contains exactly one agent. In keeping with the earlier demand analysis, there must be seventeen Cache PU and fourteen Monitor Claim Processing PU processing units to support the anticipated volume of activity.

Clusters

Clusters are the highest level of organization for TIBCO BusinessEvents. To some extent your choice of which agents to use will determine the minimum number of clusters needed. For example, if you decide to use both process agents and inference agents, you have no choice other than to use at least two clusters since the two cannot be mixed in the same cluster (see Chapter 8).

More commonly, however, your decision to use multiple clusters will be driven by performance considerations. By default, communications between cache agents and other agents within a cluster occur via the multicast address that defines the cluster. If your solution involves cache objects that are unrelated to one another and share no logic, there is a performance advantage to using a different cluster for each group of cache objects and their related logic. Channels can then be used for communications between the clusters. This is the rationale for

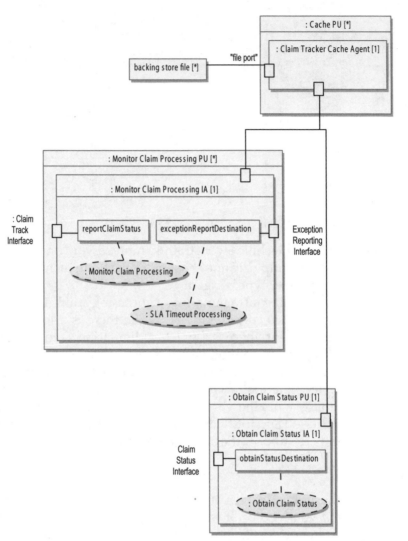

Figure 17-5: *Claim Tracker Processing Unit Modularization*

separating monitoring solutions (BEMM, in particular) into separate clusters (Figure 17-5). Similarly, if the Claim Tracker were monitoring processes that were also executing in TIBCO BusinessEvents, it would be good practice to deploy the Claim Tracker in its own cluster.

Object Management Configuration

Your choice of object management modes for the various objects in your design will impact the detailed design of rule functions and determine the need for clean-up rules. Thus it is important that these decisions be made early in the design process and be clearly understood by those implementing your design.

There are three categories of decisions to be made for the objects in your design: the object management mode, the degree of replication, and the use and mode of backing store. The cluster deployment descriptor defines the defaults for each and, by exception, allows you to override the object management mode and use of backing store for selected objects.

Object Management Mode

Generally, the best choice is to make Cache Only the default mode, and by exception specify the objects that use other modes. This is the preferred choice for concepts.

For events, there is a choice to be made depending upon the role that the event plays. If the event is purely a trigger and will not be needed later, Cache Only is a reasonable choice. The event is automatically removed from the agent working memory at the end of the RTC cycle.

Events, however, sometimes serve as data elements that are used in subsequent processing. In such cases, Memory Only is the appropriate mode to choose. With this mode, the object will remain in working memory until it is explicitly removed or its time-to-live expires. In all cases, when you choose Memory Only mode for an object you must also specify the logic for its removal from working memory.

Note that when a concept is contained within another concept the object management modes for both must be the same.

Object Replication

For objects in Cache Only mode, you have the option of creating in-memory backup copies. This provides a level of fault tolerance against the failure of individual cache agents, but does not protect against failures that cause the entire set of cache agents to shut down. You can also specify the minimum number of cache agents that must be operational before the agents using the cache will start. Note that this constraint only applies at start-up.

Backing Store

The backing store provides persistence for the objects in the cache. A single choice applies to the entire cluster, but individual objects can be marked as not being saved in the backing store. The configuration choices are

- No backing store
- Shared all (database) with cache-aside
- Shared all (database) with write-behind
- Shared nothing (file)

Your choice of backing store approach determines the kind of potential inconsistencies that may arise when agents are terminated unexpectedly. Because this affects the detail of design, the backing store decisions should be made before any detailed design is done.

Claim Tracker Object Management Configuration

Table 17-1 shows the object management configuration for the Claim Tracker example. Since the Claim Tracker is not the system of record for status information (it exists to speed up the location of a claim and accelerate the identification of processing problems), fault tolerance is not a requirement and therefore there will be no replication. Due to the volume of activity, Shared-Nothing backing store is selected for efficiency. Inbound events serve only as triggers, and outbound events are not needed once sent, so all events are managed in Memory Only mode. The Claim Status and Status Report concepts are managed Cache Only.

Table 17-1: *Claim Tracker Object Management Configuration*

Object	Management Mode	Replication	Backing Store
Claim Status concept	Cache Only	none	Shared Nothing
Status Report concept	Cache Only	none	Shared Nothing
Claim Status Notification event	Memory Only, ttl=0	none	none
Claim Processing Exception event	Memory Only, ttl=0	none	none
Claim Status Request event	Memory Only, ttl=0	none	none
Claim Status Response event	Memory Only, ttl=0	none	none

Deployment Patterns

The performance analysis you have performed and modularization decisions you have made are not, in themselves, sufficient to ensure that your solution, when deployed, will meet the performance goals. In order to ensure this, you need to indicate your intent with regard to the deployment of the solution components on machines, indicating which components can share machines and which should be on separate machines. You should also indicate the minimum class of machine required.

While the deployment pattern may be trivial, it is important to clearly communicate your design intent in terms of how the application should be deployed. Figure 17-6 shows the intended deployment for the Claim Tracker solution. This clearly shows that each processing unit should be deployed on a separate machine.

Table 17-2 shows the intended configuration for each machine used in the Claim Tracker deployment pattern and the number of each that will be required.

In addition to specifying the initial deployment, it is prudent to give guidelines on how capacity can be scaled. In the Claim Tracker example, each Cache Machine is holding the status information for 4.26 million claims. The initially deployed capacity is thus 76.7 million claims, and the initial demand is expected to be for 70.4 million claims. As the demand begins to approach the deployed capacity, additional Cache Machines can be deployed, each adding a capacity of 4.26 million claims.

Similarly, each Monitoring Machine can process 425 events/second, giving a capacity of 5,950 events/second. Initial demand is expected to be 5,356 events/second (4,736 normal events + 620 timeout events). As demand grows, Monitoring Machines can be added, each adding a capacity of 425 events/second.

Table 17-2: *Claim Tracker Machine Configuration*

Machine	RAM	CPU	Number Required
Monitoring Machine	16GB	8 core	14
Cache Machine	64GB	8 core	18
Claim Status Machine	16GB	8 core	1
EMS Machine	8GB	4 core	1

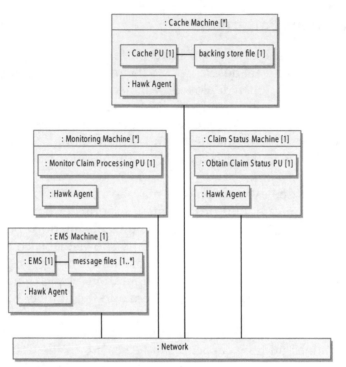

Figure 17-6: *Claim Tracker Deployment*

The EMS server, properly configured, should be able to handle 10,000 messages/second with asynchronous persistence. The initial solution demand will be 5,356 messages/second. It is not anticipated that the message volume will exceed the capacity of the server. Should this occur, message traffic would have to be partitioned.

Some of the EMS message traffic is coming from business partners. Further design is required for the business partner communication.

Deployment Requirements for Run-Time Configurability

Rule templates and decision tables provide the ability to modify decision logic at runtime. However, doing so requires the deployment of the Rule Management Server. The Rule Management Server has its own CDD file and runs as a separate cluster. Its deployment must be planned as with any other cluster.

Another option for supporting run-time changes is to select Hot Deployment on the processing unit configuration in the solution's CDD file. When this box is checked, the processing unit monitors the EAR files for changes. If it discovers a change, it halts inference agents at the end of the RTC cycle, loads the changes, and resumes execution.

The types of changes that are supported for hot deployment are limited. You can't, for example, add a state machine to an existing concept, as this would change existing instances of the concept. Consult the *TIBCO BusinessEvents® Administration* manual for the specifics regarding allowed types of changes.

Monitoring

An important part of deployment planning is the determination of the monitoring that will be required for the solution. It almost goes without saying that liveness monitoring of the individual executables is a requirement. In addition, there should be monitoring to indicate when the solution is getting into performance trouble. This monitoring should indicate whether service-level agreements are being met and further track whether actual activity volumes remain within the planned-for bounds.

The architect's tasks in this regard are to

- Identify the measurements that need to be made
- Define the mechanism(s) for making the required measurements
- Define the mechanism(s) for determining whether the measurements lie within expected bounds
- Define the mechanism(s) for alerting personnel when measurements exceed the bounds

For the Claim Tracker solution, the rate at which events are being processed is a key indicator of both the solution's ability to keep up with demand and the demand itself. A secondary measure is the backlog of `Claim Status Notification` events waiting to be processed.

To make the measurement of the event processing rate, a Monitoring Scorecard is used (Figure 17-7). Each `Monitor Claim Processing IA` inference agent has its own instance of this scorecard. The preprocessing

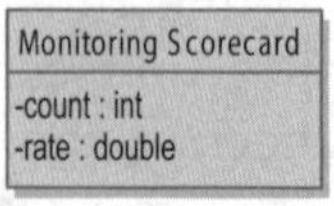

Figure 17-7: *Monitoring Scorecard*

for each `Claim Status Notification` event increments the `count`. A timer event periodically (say, every five minutes) reads the count, updates the rate, and resets the count to zero. Thus each agent has a scorecard containing the current rate at which events are being processed.

The TIBCO Hawk® agent running on each `Monitoring Machine` uses the Hawk microagent embedded in the `Monitor Claim Processing PU` to periodically read the rate and compare it against a preestablished performance threshold (e.g., 425 events/second) and sends an alert if the threshold is exceeded.

The TIBCO Hawk agent running on the `EMS Machine` monitors the `ReportClaimStatus` queue and sends an alert if the queue backlog exceeds a preestablished threshold (e.g., 20,000 events).

Further design is required to connect the Hawk alerts to the customer's system monitoring solution.

Summary

Functionality in TIBCO BusinessEvents solutions can be modularized at three different levels: cluster, processing unit, and agent. At the agent level, different classes of agents can be defined, each executing a subset of the functionality. These agent classes are then grouped into processing units, each of which represents a JVM configuration. Finally, each cluster contains a number of processing unit configurations.

Partitioning functionality into different processing units sets the stage for scaling and tuning the solution. When different processing units are deployed on different machines, you can be assured that they will not compete with one another for machine resources.

Multiple clusters may be required for technical or performance reasons. Inference and process agents, for example, cannot be run in the same cluster. Monitoring solutions (BEMM, for example) are usually run in a separate cluster from the solution they are monitoring so that monitoring resource demands do not adversely impact the solution being monitored.

The configuration of object management impacts the detailed design of rules and rule functions. Because of this, it is good practice to define the object management mode, replication, and backing store for each type of object before detailed design is started.

The need to change logic at runtime impacts both detailed design and deployment. If rule templates or decision tables are to be used, the logic to be changed must be represented using these constructs. Furthermore, the Rule Management Server must be deployed as part of the solution to enable the run-time changes. Another approach is to enable processing units to pick up changes at runtime by monitoring the EAR file for changes. However, there are restrictions as to the types of changes that can be accommodated with this approach.

The architect needs to specify the intended run-time deployment pattern for the solution. This should indicate the different machine types required, what is installed on each, and the number of each that will be required. The manner in which the solution will be monitored should also be defined.

Chapter 18

Fault Tolerance, High Availability, and Site Disaster Recovery

Objectives

When the functions being performed by a complex-event processing solution become mission critical, the availability and reliability of the solution need to be considered. This chapter discusses the available options provided by TIBCO BusinessEvents®. Options for other TIBCO components, such as TIBCO Enterprise Message Service™, are covered in *Architecting Composite Applications and Services with TIBCO®*.[1]

After reading this chapter, you will be able to describe

- How a fault-tolerant solution can be architected with TIBCO BusinessEvents
- How non-cache agents can be configured for high availability
- How cache agents can be configured for fault tolerance and site disaster recovery

---

1. Paul C. Brown, *Architecting Composite Applications and Services with TIBCO®*, Boston: Addison-Wesley (2012).

Solution Fault Tolerance

Fault tolerance in TIBCO BusinessEvents® solutions depends upon a number of things:

- The cache's backing store configuration
- The use of appropriate coordination patterns
- The use of JMS channels with persistence for interactions between agents
- The use of appropriate fault-tolerance patterns for the JMS message service when it is being used as a transport
- The use of a fault-tolerant database configuration when a database is being used as the backing store
- The use of a fault-tolerant storage subsystem when files are being used as the backing store

Backing Store Configuration for Fault Tolerance

There are two backing store configurations that can support fault tolerance:

1. Shared All Cache Aside
2. Shared Nothing with SYNC persistence policy

With both of these configurations, when an inference agent does a cache update prior to acknowledging the receipt of a request, the persistence of information in the backing store is confirmed as part of the operation. Thus the acknowledgment indicates successful persistence.

Coordination Patterns

Inference, query, and process agents are not fault tolerant. At best, depending upon their configuration, they are highly available. Because of this, the coordination patterns in which they participate are critical to achieving overall fault-tolerant behavior.

There are two principal coordination patterns, depending upon the type of transport being used for the event. If the solution uses HTTP, TCP, or other type of transport that does not itself persist the event, the request-reply pattern of Figure 18-1 must be used. In this pattern the requesting party sends a request and waits for a reply. The agent

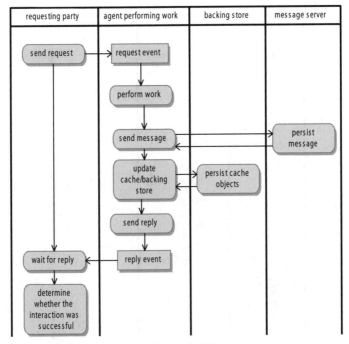

| requesting party | agent performing work | backing store | message server |

Figure 18-1: *Request-Reply Pattern for Fault Tolerance*

performing the work does the work, sends any required messages, updates the cache and backing store, and only then returns the reply.

With this pattern, the reply indicates not only that the initial work has been accomplished but also that any cache updates and required messages have been performed in a manner that will survive the shutdown of any software components. This pattern places an obligation on the requesting party to confirm that the interaction was successful and take appropriate action if it was not. The most common action is to resend the request.

The fact that the request might be resent must be considered in the design of the agent's work performance. If there are non-idempotent activities (activities that cannot be repeated), the agent must have logic to determine whether these activities have already been performed and alternative logic to handle the case when they have.

The other coordination pattern is used when the source of the event is a JMS message server (Figure 18-2). This pattern is similar to the previous one. The difference is that the message server already has logic to handle the case in which the message is not acknowledged: It will re-deliver the message. This pattern requires that the JMS destination

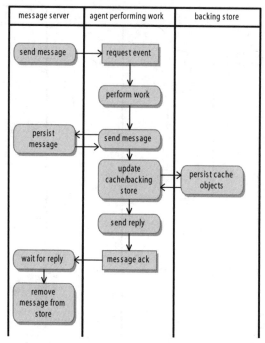

Figure 18-2: *Persistent Event Pattern for Fault Tolerance*

use the EXPLICIT CLIENT ACKNOWLEDGE mode. This ensures that the acknowledgment is not sent until all pending cache updates are complete and pending messages have been sent.

Inter-Agent Communications

The third design requirement is that all inter-agent communications use JMS messaging. This ensures that messages are not lost. In particular, you do not want to use local channels for communications between agents. With local channels, any failure that occurs between the time a message is sent and the completion of the work, cache update, and outbound message sending will result in a loss of work-in-progress.

Site Disaster Recovery

Enabling the solution for site disaster recovery requires a storage subsystem behind the cache and messaging server to replicate the files between the sites. If the solution fault-tolerance guidelines just discussed are followed, all necessary state information is in these files, and the solution can be recovered at the remote site.

Summary

Creating a fault-tolerant solution with TIBCO BusinessEvents requires the use of appropriate backing store configurations, the use of the TIBCO Enterprise Message Service with message persistence, and the use of appropriate coordination patterns for agent work. Persistent messaging must be used for all inter-agent interactions.

Site disaster recovery requires that the storage subsystem replicate the files underlying both the backing store and the message service to the remote site.

Chapter 19

Best Practices

Objectives

Putting together a robust complex-event processing solution can be straightforward if certain best practices are followed. This chapter provides an overview of those best practices. After this chapter you will be able to describe

- Architecture planning
- Testing best practices
- Data model design best practices
- Rule design best practices
- Object management modes, locking, and threading

Architecture Planning

A well-considered architecture is the key to success in complex-event processing. Don't guess. Use the checklist from Chapter 3 to determine whether you are prepared.

- Is the information related to the problem understood well enough to create a quality information model (including relevant state information)?

- Is there a well-defined (i.e., measurable) set of criteria that defines the situation that needs to be recognized?
- Are there well-defined triggers that identify the points in time at which the situation recognition analysis will be performed?
- Is the information necessary for this recognition analysis readily accessible?
- Is there a clearly articulated approach for using the available information to recognize the situation?
- Is there a well-defined (i.e., measurable) approach for responding to the situation once it has been recognized?
- Is the reference information needed for determining the response readily accessible?
- Does the business value of the resulting situation recognition and response capabilities warrant the investment in the solution?

If you answered yes to all of these questions, you are well positioned to select or define a sound architecture for your solution.

If, on the other hand, you answered no to any of these questions, you have some preliminary work to do, both analytical and experimental. Approach the problem iteratively. Do some analysis to gain insight on how the problem might be tackled. Do an experiment to verify that the approach is practical. Keep iterating until you have solid answers to all of the previous questions.

Focus first on the aspect of the problem with greatest uncertainty. Consider the concept data model first, particularly when there is a state machine involved. Next, consider the events that drive the changes to the concepts and state machines. Finally, structure the rules and rule functions necessary to execute the changes. And consider how you are going to convince yourself you got it right!

Designing Data Models for Concepts

As much as possible, break down your data model into small, independent groups of concepts. Having large interrelated groups of concepts will require a lot of work to update rules and rule functions when you make changes. Use events to communicate facts from one block of rules to another. The modularization patterns described in Chapter 13 are good examples to follow. This will ease the maintenance of your design.

Object Management Modes, Threading, and Locking

There are three highly interdependent architectural choices that you have to make in every project: selecting the object management mode for each object, selecting a threading model for each destination, and establishing a locking policy for each object. Your choice of combination for each object type and destination will have a far-reaching impact on the implementation details for your solution. These choices should be made—and validated through analysis—early in the project. A significant portion of your testing should be devoted to ensuring that locking policies have been correctly implemented and that there are no problems related to race conditions. These kinds of problems are nearly impossible to troubleshoot in a deployed system. They warrant a solid testing investment.

Designing Rules

Keep your rules simple.

- Keep the number of concepts in a condition to a minimum for efficiency. Remember that multiple concepts require a join, and joins are expensive operations.
- Avoid complex conditions.
- Choose multiple simple rules with intermediate events rather than one complex rule.

These guidelines extend to the application as a whole. In complicated situations, draw an intermediate conclusion and announce it as an event. Then use this event to trigger further analysis. If necessary, you can use a transient concept to convey information between rules. A transient concept is one that is defined with Memory Only management.

Remember that the structure of your condition clauses impacts performance. Use filters whenever possible to narrow down the number of objects that will be tried in subsequent join clauses. Similarly, use equivalent joins to further reduce the number of objects that will be tried in nonequivalent joins. The more objects involved, the more important this becomes.

Testing Best Practices

Understanding the behavior of rule-based systems has always been a challenge. Because of this, it is good practice when writing rules to do the following:

- Clearly define the behavior you are expecting for each block of functionality you implement (rule table, collection of rules and rule functions, process design, etc.).
- Define how you are going to convince yourself that you have attained the expected behavior.
- Implement test scenarios to verify the expected behavior.

Remember that the behavior you are specifying consists of both cache updates and outbound events. Be sure to test the entire life cycle of objects: creation, modification, and deletion. If the behavior depends upon the current state of information, whether in cache or elsewhere, determine how you are going to create this state for the beginning of the test, and how you are going to examine the state at the end of the test.

While this level of testing may seem to be a lot of work, it usually turns out to be less work than unraveling why your overall solution is not doing what you intended.

Summary

Complex-event processing solutions are ... complex! There's a lot going on, usually in parallel, and many details to consider. It is very easy to get lost in the details. To avoid getting lost, it is imperative that you keep the big picture in focus. It is the architecture of your solution that defines this big picture. It must be clearly articulated and thoroughly understood before anyone dives into the details of writing rules and rule functions.

First, make sure your problem is well defined and well understood. Uncertainty at this level is a recipe for chaos. Once the objectives and approach are defined, think data first: What information is in the events, and what reference data is required to analyze those events? How much of that reference data is dynamically updated by the event stream? What metadata (e.g., state models of processes) is required for analysis?

Once the data is understood, now consider how the processing of the data will be organized. Which processing streams will occur in parallel? What object locking will be required? What object management modes will be used?

When designing rules, keep in mind that the rule condition structure can have a significant impact on performance. In general, simple is better.

Finally, test, test, and then test again—(particularly exploring corner conditions). Rule-based approaches and parallel processing are both notorious for exhibiting unexpected behavior, particularly for the corner cases. Do your due diligence, and you will have an exemplary solution that provides your enterprise with valuable capabilities!

Index

A

Account Change Recognition, 151–152
Actions
    partitioning situation recognition from
        response, 188–189
    rule agenda, 81
    rule clauses of inference agents, 78–79
    sequential and conditional, 157–160
    synchronous I/O calls in rule actions, 231
Active sensing, 6–7
ActiveMatrix
    BPM, 49–50, 159
    BusinessWorks. *See* BusinessWorks
    database adapter. *See* Adapter for
        Database
    integration with, 172
    process orchestration and, 49–50, 159
    resource information for, 171
    Service Grid, 204
ActiveMatrix BPM, 49–50, 159
ActiveSpaces
    channel types, 88
    Data Grid and, 160
Adapter for Database
    database interaction with, 182–183
    Inference Agent Publication pattern, 183
    Inference Agent Request-Reply pattern,
        183
    Inference Agent Subscription pattern,
        184–185
    updating reference data on external
        system, 147
Administrator, TIBCO, 56, 68
Agents
    cache agents. *See* cache agents
    dashboard agents. *See* dashboard agents
    deadlocks and, 199
    in deployment, 241–242
    directing related work to single agent,
        202–203

inference agents. *See* inference agents
inter-agent communications, 256
modularization and, 240–241
options for turning on profiler, 226
partitioning and, 188–189
process agents. *See* process agents
processing units and, 243
query agents. *See* query agents
TIBCO BusinessEvents, 56
types of, 63–64
Alerts, display options, 137
Analysis. *See also* sense-analyze-respond
    pattern
    approaches to event analysis, 25–26
    capabilities of event-enabled enterprises,
        31–32
    CEP (complex-event processing) and,
        17–19
    complex events requiring, 16–17
    context required for event analysis, 23–24
    correlation in, 21
    event-enabled enterprises and, 11
    inference agents and, 69
    innovations in, 8
    interpreting, 236
    of performance, 234–236
    rule-based, 19–20
    Track-and-Trace pattern and, 43
    triggers for, 261
*Architecting Composite Applications and Services
    with TIBCO* (Brown), *xx*, 171, 203
Architecture
    best practices for planning, 259–260
    Nouveau Health Care case study, 213–214
    variability of CEP architectures, 36
Asynchronous Service Consumer pattern
    interaction with BusinessWorks, 185
    TIBCO BusinessEvents as service
        consumer, 175–178
`attribute` keyword, 77

TIBCO Education

You've read the book... now take action!
TIBCO Education is offering intense companion courses and a professional certification for each of the books in the architecture series from TIBCO Press. Each course will be released to coincide with the publication of its companion book. The planned series includes:

- **ARC 701:** TIBCO Architecture Fundamentals (available now)

- **ARC 702:** Architecting Composite Applications and Services with TIBCO (available now)

- **ARC 703:** Architecting BPM Solutions with TIBCO

- **ARC 704:** Architecting Complex Event Processing Solutions with TIBCO (available now)

- **ARC 705:** Architecting Data Centric Solutions with TIBCO

Accelerate your career with TIBCO Certification.
TIBCO Certified Architect certifications are the highest level of accreditation in the TIBCO Certified Professional Program. These prestigious credentials recognize those individuals who demonstrate a clear understanding of the selected TIBCO products, a sound grasp of architecture concepts, methodology, and principles and how they may be combined to solve practical or challenging requirements.

To learn more about the courses and certification, visit the TIBCO Education website at http://www.tibco.com/services/educational

Safari
Books Online

FREE
Online Edition

Your purchase of **Architecting Complex-Event Processing Solutions with TIBCO®** includes access to a free online edition for 45 days through the **Safari Books Online** subscription service. Nearly every Addison-Wesley Professional book is available online through **Safari Books Online**, along with thousands of books and videos from publishers such as Cisco Press, Exam Cram, IBM Press, O'Reilly Media, Prentice Hall, Que, Sams, and VMware Press.

Safari Books Online is a digital library providing searchable, on-demand access to thousands of technology, digital media, and professional development books and videos from leading publishers. With one monthly or yearly subscription price, you get unlimited access to learning tools and information on topics including mobile app and software development, tips and tricks on using your favorite gadgets, networking, project management, graphic design, and much more.

Activate your FREE Online Edition at
informit.com/safarifree

STEP 1: Enter the coupon code: MLCMMXA.

STEP 2: New Safari users, complete the brief registration form.
Safari subscribers, just log in.

If you have difficulty registering on Safari or accessing the online edition,
please e-mail customer-service@safaribooksonline.com